Friends Forever

J. P. Vaswani

GITA PUBLISHING HOUSE
Sadhu Vaswani Mission,
10, Sadhu Vaswani Path,
Pune - 411 001, (India).
gph@sadhuvaswani.org

FRIENDS FOREVER

©2013, J. P. Vaswani

ISBN: 978-93-80743-77-6

Sadhu Vaswani Mission,
10, Sadhu Vaswani Path, Pune - 411 001, (India).
gph@sadhuvaswani.org

Printed by:
MEHTA OFFSET PVT. LTD.
Mehta House,
A-16, Naraina Industrial Area Phase-II,
New Delhi - 110 028. (India).
info@mehtaoffset.com

Friends Forever

J. P. Vaswani

Gita Publishing House,
PUNE, (India).
www.dadavaswanisbooks.org

Books and Booklets by J.P. Vaswani

7 Commandments of the Bhagavad Gita

10 Commandments of a Successful Marriage

100 Stories You Will Never Forget

108 Pearls of Practical Wisdom

108 Simple Prayers of a Simple Man

108 Thoughts on Success

114 Thoughts on Love

A Little Book of Life

A Little Book of Wisdom

A Simple and Easy Way To God

A Treasure of Quotes

Around The Camp Fire

Be In The Driver's Seat

Be An Achiever

Begin the Day with God

Bhagavad Gita in a Nutshell

Burn Anger Before Anger Burns You

Comrades of God - Lives of Saints from East & West

Daily Appointment with God

Daily Inspiration (A Thought For Every Day Of The Year)

Daily Inspiration

Destination Happiness

Dewdrops of Love

Does God Have Favorites

Finding Peace of Mind

Formula for Prosperity

Gateways to Heaven

God In Quest of Man

Good Parenting

How to Overcome Depression

I am a Sindhi

I Luv U, God!

Joy Peace Pills

Kill Fear Before Fear Kills You

Ladder of Abhyasa

Lessons Life Has Taught Me

Life after Death

Life and Teachings of Sadhu Vaswani

Life and Teachings of the Sikh Gurus

Living in the Now

Management Moment by Moment

Mantra for the Modern Man

Mantras For Peace Of Mind

Many Scriptures: One Wisdom

Many Paths: One Goal

Nearer, My God, To Thee!

New Education Can Make the World New

Peace or Perish: There Is No Other Choice

Positive Power of Thanksgiving

Questions Answered

Saints For You and Me

Saints With A Difference

Say No to Negatives

Secrets of Health And Happiness

Shake Hands With Life

Short Sketches of Saints Known & Unknown

Sketches of Saints Known & Unknown

Spirituality in Daily Life

Stop Complaining: Start Thanking!

Swallow Irritation Before Irritation Swallows You

Teachers are Sculptors

The Goal Of Life and How To Attain It

The Highway to Happiness

The Little Book of Freedom from Stress

The Little Book of Prayer

The Little Book of Service

The Little Book of Success

The Little Book of Yoga

The Magic of Forgiveness

The Miracle of Forgiving

The New Age Diet: Vegetarianism for You and Me

The Perfect Relationship: Guru and Disciple

The Terror Within

The Way of Abhyasa (How To Meditate)

Thus Have I Been Taught

Tips For Teenagers

What You Would Like To Know About Karma?

What You Would Like To know About Hinduism?

What To Do When Difficulties Strike?

Why Do Good People Suffer?

Women: Where Would The World Be Without You?

Why Be Sad?

You Are Not Alone: God Is With You!

You Can Change Your Life

Contents

Section I

SECTION II - How to Make Good Friends and Keep Them

Chapter 1

What is Friendship?

As Dear to Me as My Brother...

We know and adore Sri Rama as the ideal son, the ideal prince, the ideal husband and the perfect man, indeed, as *Maryada Purushottama*, the perfect man of virtue. But the Ramayana also tells us of his qualities as an ideal friend.

When Sri Rama leaves Ayodhya as an exile, the first outsider whom he meets is Guha, hunter and tribesman, King of the *Nishadas*. His capital, Sringiberapura, is situated on the banks of the Ganga; Sri Rama is determined to cross the river and begin his *vanvaas* in the dense forests on the other bank, so that the people of Ayodhya might not follow him. All he needs is a boat to ferry him across the Ganga, along with Lakshmana and Sita. The meeting of Sri Rama with Guha is described not only in the Valmiki Ramayana but also in the Kamba Ramayana in Tamil. The poet Kambar idealises Guha as the true friend and the Lord's great affection for him is depicted in beautiful terms.

On hearing that Sri Rama has arrived in his kingdom, Guha rushes to greet him and welcome him with the choicest foods from his land. Sri Rama embraces him affectionately and enquires after the welfare of his kingdom and his people; politely and kindly, he tells Guha that he cannot accept the fine delicacies brought to him, for he is now beginning his life as an ascetic in the forest. He declines Guha's offer of hospitality, and having taken a drink of water, he goes to sleep under a tree on the banks of the river.

Guha is devastated at the sight of his Lord sleeping out in the open; his grief knows no bounds when Lakshmana explains to him about Kaikeyi's designs and Rama's decision to leave Ayodhya. He stays awake all night, keeping vigil with Lakshmana to guard Rama and Sita.

Next morning, Sri Rama requests him to help with a boat that may ferry them across the river. Guha begs him to stay with his people at Sringiberapura; "My people and I will happily live under your dispensation," he tells Sri Rama. Rama lovingly returns the kingdom so graciously offered to him, and bids Guha rule over his people with justice and compassion. Guha then begs Rama to permit him and his soldiers to accompany them into the forest, so that they may serve him during the long fourteen-year exile. Gently, Sri Rama reminds him that the conditions of ascetic life are now binding on him, and that Guha's loving offer cannot be accepted. The great poet Kambar, expresses Sri Rama's loving friendship in immortal words by making Sri Rama say: "With you, we are now five brothers, not four!"

Later, when Bharata arrives at Sringiberapura with the mighty army of Ayodhya and all the people of the city following him to persuade Rama to go back to Ayodhya with them, Guha is at first disturbed on seeing him; Guha's fear is that Bharata might want to harm his brother, in order to secure the kingdom; but Bharata assures him that he has come to surrender himself and the Kingdom at Sri Rama's feet and to take him back to Ayodhya. Guha is happy and relieved to hear this and embraces Bharata with joy. Bharata, too, rejoices that his elder brother should be blessed with such a noble friend.

To complete this beautiful story of friendship, we are told that when Sri Rama was about to return to Ayodhya after vanquishing Ravana (which was actually the purpose of his *avatara*) he sent Hanuman before him to inform Guha and Bharata of his impending return. "Guha will be pleased to hear about my welfare and safe return," says Sri Rama, "for he is a dear friend to me, and holds me as dear as the self."

The Lord demonstrates the ideal of friendship that is selfless and undemanding, expects no material benefits, transcends all barriers of class, caste and social status, and yet sustains the highest values of mutual care and affection in the beautiful friendship that he shares with Guha.

Mitra in the Vedas and Avesta

"...the word (Mitra) also means a friend ...and the kindly nature of God is often referred to in the Veda, Mitra even appearing as the god of peace... while in the Avesta, Mitra is on the ethical side of his character the guardian of faithfulness...(the word) must have originally signified 'ally' or 'friend' and have been applied to the sun-god in his aspect of a beneficent power of nature".

Mac Donell, *History of Vedic Mythology*

What is Friendship?

There can be as many answers to that question as there are friends in this world, and I'm sure there are very many of them!

Friendship is not easy to define or even describe. Companionship, camaraderie, fellowship, amity, these may be good synonyms as far as dictionary use is concerned, but friendship is something special, for those who are blessed with it! I am told that the Eskimos have a hundred different words for snow. How I wish the English language could offer us those many options for the words that we use so lovingly! All we have are adjectives to describe different kinds of friends, such as close friend, best friend, childhood friend, school friend, trusted friend and so on.

But friendship is special to all of us and friends are special people in our lives. It was a wise man who pointed out, "We can't pick or choose our family, and we are always severely limited in the number of our family members. Social norms and our own morals demand that our spouse is no more than one. But there's no limit to the number of friends we can choose and keep for life!" We can have as many friends as there are adjectives to describe them; I have come across 'school friends', 'college friends', 'train friends', 'golf friends', 'work friends' and even 'coffee break friends'! Truth to tell, our friends reflect the diverse choices we make in life.

Two thousand five hundred years ago, Aristotle defined true friends as one soul in two bodies. I wonder how many of us will accept such a definition today. But there is something in his words that still holds good for all of us: we look to our friends not just to complement us, but in a sense to complete something that may be missing in us. There is a void in our lives which only friendship can fill.

In the good old days, friendship was thought to be essential to the good of both the individual and society. Many wise kings and great leaders chose wise writers and philosophers to be their friends, so that the state could benefit from their wisdom and experience. "Wise friends make you wise," says the Book of Proverbs. The philosopher Epicurus actually cited wisdom and friendship as the twin goals of a well-lived life. Aristotle stated that friendship was one of those 'virtues' that constituted human happiness. Thus, friendship was an important element in a network of social relationships which formed the very fabric of early communities. Early Christians lived in communities of friends, for reasons of safety and moral support. Such friendship was pragmatic as well as affectionate; it involved mutual cooperation as well as interpersonal feelings of loyalty, reciprocity and obligation.

However, many modern thinkers feel that in those early days, this element of 'reciprocity' involved military understanding, i.e. the commonly expressed notion that my enemy's enemy is my friend, because we can get together and defeat our common enemy. It was for such a reason that sworn enemies Britain and France actually became 'allies' to defeat the common enemy, Germany, during World War II. I might add too, in a lighter vein, that British Prime Minister Winston Churchill, who was fiercely anti-Communist, justified British support to the Soviet forces in the same war; when he was questioned in Parliament about his change of heart, he is said to have declared that, "if Hitler invaded Hell, I would make at least a favourable reference to the Devil in the House of Commons," in support of British aid to Soviet forces. In the 21st Century, we have a cartoonist denying such utilitarian reasons for friendship by his famous maxim: "The enemy of my enemy is my enemy's enemy; no more, no less". They say that it is only in the last few centuries that the quality of disinterestedness has become important in friendship: that is, people do not really expect to 'benefit' in material terms out of their true friends. Ideally, friendship should transcend such selfish considerations.

A young lady who is one of our Mission volunteers once said to me that her life would be unbearable without her close friends; this might not be surprising in itself, but for the fact that none of her really close friends lived anywhere 'close' to her geographically; she agreed that it would be very good if they could meet often and spend time in each other's company; however, none of them felt each other's absence as they were in constant touch with one another by means of those communication devices and networks which have really shrunk the world!

Skype, Blackberry, Whatsapp… friendship is just a touch away with modern digital devices, the young lady said with a smile. Indeed, the post-modern era we live in has added a new dimension to long-distance friendship! I was glad to hear her views, for I had recently read a research study which claimed that personal friendships are on the decline, with people having fewer confidants or social companions with whom they spend time sharing interests or activities or even 'opening up' to one another. The reason cited was ironic: people are spending more and more time with their gadgets which leaves them with far less time for actual, human, interpersonal communication. We are on Facebook and Twitter and Linked in and a dozen other internet 'groups' and 'forums'. But we have no time for friends!

Can you form lasting friendships on Facebook? Can 'virtual' or 'internet' friendships replace good old practices of meeting, greeting and breaking bread together? Yes, say millions of people who live their social lives on the web – and not just youngsters, but also many senior citizens, for whom net 'groups' and 'forums' offer iendship through the keyboard and computer screen. Can endless chats on Skype ad BBM substitute face-to-face conversations, laughing together and slapping ach other on the back? I am not going to answer these questions!

recent research study in Britain has concluded that incivility, rudeness and abusive nguage is growing on social networking sites. Online friendships are being cut ort after virtual spats and fierce rows! People who would never call their friends ames in person, are freely doing so on the net, the study tells us. On the other hand, yalists of the virtual world assert that cyberspace is full of lively, intelligent people any of whom share your views and attitudes and it is possible for us to make good iends who actually have a lot in common with us!

ir Francis Bacon, the Renaissance scholar and writer did not mince words when he egan his famous essay "Of Friendship" with the words: "Whatsoever (whosoever) delighted in solitude, is either a wild beast or a God." We may note that Bacon does ot devalue solitude. He goes on to add that solitude is good for reflection and ontemplation when one sets out to discover the higher truths of life: but in the veryday life of the society and community, one who lacks good friends is indeed a eprived being! I dare say Bacon would take a different view if he realised that you eed the solitude of your own secluded space to seek the company of your friends on igital devices!

oud chatter and laughter in noisy company is not what friendship is all about! "For crowd is not company; and faces are but a gallery of pictures; and talk but a tinkling ymbal, where there is no love," according to Bacon. Love and affection then, are that friendship is all about; as also trust, loyalty, honesty and truth. In fact, even hared activities and interests need not be necessary; good friends can be as different s the proverbial chalk and cheese. And 'hanging out together' or 'doing things ogether' is not for all ages and all types of people. Volunteers who serve the same ause; understanding colleagues at the workplace; people who meet regularly at a ospital for their treatment; even commuters who share the same public transport an become good friends, or stay strangers to each other!

here are many people who will tell you, "My husband/wife/mother/daughter/son is ay best friend!" Who are we to quarrel with this idea? Such people have gone eyond the idea of dividing their life into family and non-family compartments, and ound trust, loyalty and companionship in their closest family members.

And then, there is the very American notion of 'family': i.e. friends who are so close nit that they have become part of an extended network of relationships, just like the ood old extended family.

We have used the word 'friendship' extensively, but what does it really mean? Who a close friend? Researchers asked two generations, male and female, to say wh they thought of this concept:

Many working women felt that a close friend was someone you could get on real well with, who was always ready to help you when you had problems, who gives yo sound advice, and who always had time for you. Quite a few of them said that the were too shy or withdrawn to make good friends in school or college, but coming o to work enabled them to have good friends. Significantly, many of them felt that was difficult to have a 'close friend' of the opposite sex.

Some people felt that a close friend could only be someone whom they had know for a long time, and whom they could still get on with. Theirs was a friendship tha had stood the test of time. Quite a few in this group shared similar hobbies, so tha they shared activities together. They took vacations with their friends; went campin or trekking together; or just spent time in outdoor activities.

A large number of people confessed that they did not really have any close friend Of course, they knew a lot of people, either through work or through socia occasions. But they hesitated to describe acquaintances and people they knew a 'friends'.

Many people felt that if one comes from a close-knit family, then friends are actuall superfluous. The little free time they had, they preferred to spend with their family.

For young adults, close friends were the people they preferred to spend all their fre time with. They lived in close proximity to their friends, and met each other ofte They were not doing the same thing, that is, some of them were at college, some c them were working and some of them were yet to choose their careers. But, the preferred to spend time in each other's company. "I can do without my family for month or two, but I can't dream of being without my friends," was how one of the put it.

Friendship is one of the greatest blessings that we can enjoy in life. Here is wha people had to say when they were asked to complete the sentence beginning:

Friendship is…

- Sharing joys and sorrows
- Support and encouragement when we need it most
- Loyalty and trust
- A wonderful sense of caring and sharing

- The best antidote to loneliness and despair
- The most beautiful connection outside one's ties of blood
- Companionship and participating in common activities
- Shared interests and values
- Mutual respect, affection and sympathy
- Goodwill and affection
- Shared admiration/appreciation
- Joy of pure affection, free from ulterior motives
- Complete harmony on all issues that matter
- Open and free communication without flattery or hypocrisy

I would say friendship is all this and more!

For Your Introspection

People have twice as many friends online as they do in real life, says new research. The study, found that typical users of social networking sites have 121 friends online versus 55 physical chums.

It found that one in 10 people has found their best friend online and that people tend to be more honest with friends online than when faced with friends.

"For most people, the internet is a way of keeping in touch with loved ones and friends; but for people who are isolated due to illness, it plays a more vital role and can often act as a lifeline," Helen Oxley, consultant clinical psychologist at Manchester Adult Cystic Fibrosis Centre, Wythenshawe hospital, told The Guardian.

"In wider society, the ways in which friendships are formed and nurtured is changing with people recognising that they can develop deep, meaningful connections with others that they've never met, and may never meet.

"People with illnesses often rely on the internet's ability to facilitate friendships as they blog and use networking sites as a way of coming to terms with, and dealing with their illness. It can foster a sense of social connection for those who can frequently feel isolated, which is important to psychological wellbeing."

The Guardian

Chapter 2

Who are Your Friends?

Too Many Friends, Too Few to Help

A hare was very popular with the other animals in the jungle who all claimed to be her friends. One day she heard the hounds approaching her and hoped to escape them by the aid of her friends. So, she went to the horse, and asked him to carry her away from the hounds on his back. But he declined, stating that he had important work to do for his master. "He felt sure," he said, "that all her other friends would come to her assistance." She then applied to the bull, and hoped that he would repel the hounds with his horns. The bull replied: "I am very sorry, but I have an appointment with a lady; but I feel sure that our friend, the goat will do what you want. "The goat, however, feared that his back might do her some harm if he took her upon it. The ram, he felt sure, was the proper friend to ask for help. So she went to the ram and told him the case. The ram replied: "Another time, my dear friend. I do not like to interfere on the present occasion, as hounds have been known to eat sheep as well as hares." The hare then applied, as a last hope, to the calf, who regretted that he was unable to help her, as he did not like to take the responsibility upon himself, as so many older persons than himself had declined the task. By this time the hounds were quite near, and the hare took to her heels and luckily escaped.

From *Aesop's Fables*

"True happiness consists not in the multitude of friends, but in their worth and choice."

Dr. Johnson

W e have all heard of the famous book by Dale Carnegie: How to Win Friends and Influence People. I would like to adapt that title to the theme of this chapter, your friends can win you over and influence you to a great extent. The much cited, much used saying is quite true: "Tell me who are your friends and I will tell you what you are."

This is not just true of like-minded friends who share the same interests and attitudes. Dissimilar friends can also influence you to change your way of thinking and your habits. Sometimes, this works for the better. At mutual self-help groups like Alcoholics Anonymous or even Weight Watchers Anonymous, diverse people from widely different backgrounds come together to draw support from each other to face their common problem. But they have this in common: they wish to fight their addiction; they are determined to 'kick' the bad habit that is ruining their life. Nearly everyone agrees that the group therapy and group dynamics plays a major role in achieving their goal. In other words, the company they keep influences them for their own good.

Unfortunately, the opposite holds good too. The kind of company you slip into may influence you in harmful ways. Boys and girls who leave their homes to live in a hostel, often get carried away by the sudden sense of freedom that is thrust on them. Many of them have admitted that they take to smoking or drinking due to peer pressure, as it is called.

Equally, there are young people who learn the values of hard work, dedication and commitment from their peers. Thus a lackluster, below-average student at school may fall into the company of the right friends in college who motivate him to excel in his studies or in sports.

In short, your friends can make you or break you. Therefore, it is necessary to choose them well. The friends we choose play a major role in shaping our character. Association and company also shape our social habits. Therefore the Bible tells us: "Bad Company ruins good morals." And there is also the famous proverb, "Whoever walks with the wise becomes wise, but the companion of fools will suffer harm".

Many young people are aware that the language or habits or attitude of their friends is not desirable; they know that their friends are doing the wrong thing. But they stick to the same company out of a misplaced sense of loyalty, or they fondly imagine that they themselves will be strong-willed and not fall into the same trap.

Let me ask you: if your best friend has fallen into a deep pit, what would be the best way to rescue him? Will you tumble into the same pit headlong to shout and scream for help with him? Or would you stay on the higher ground and send a rope down to pull him up? Friends with toxic habits need help from outside; you cannot get enmeshed with them and add to their woes. If you are in such a group, getting saddled with bad habits or addictions, your companions are hardly in a position to help you; you need to seek outside help; you need to change the company you keep.

Many people just stumble into the company that they find without ever exercising a choice. They do not give a thought to finding out if their friends are reliable or trustworthy or just 'good' in the old fashioned sense. They let themselves be pushed around; they do not question; they do not even think for themselves. I still remember how horrified people were when we heard the news of schoolboys in a 'gang' kidnapping and eventually murdering their classmate in the hope of getting a fat ransom from his family! When the gang was caught, the parents blamed all the other children while claiming that their own son was innocent and misled! Sheep may be very docile and mild creatures; but a sheep-like mentality is not good in friendship! And a good friend is not just one who is good to you, but good for you!

The 5 Friendship Threats

The five friendship threats that I highlight in my book, *Friendships Don't Just Happen!* are blame, jealousy, judgment, neglect and non-reciprocation.

Those five threats are the umbrella that every specific story of friendship frustration falls under, whether the judgment stems from us thinking she's dating the wrong guy or if we interpret her canceling our plans as "selfish". And, unfortunately, they can't all be avoided. The truth is that we're human, we have expectations and we have needs we want filled, so we're bound to experience these threats from time-to-time.

What we can do is be aware that some frustration and disappointment is normal in relationships, that we're just as likely to be the subject of her annoyance as she is ours, and that the most important thing in these moments is deciding how we can best respond in ways that grow our friendship.

Shasta Nelson

Friends Forever

Bad company can corrupt the best among us. Shakespeare spoke of the dyer's hand becoming 'subdued' or coloured by what it works in; you cannot dip your hands in deep, fast colours and expect them to come out clean.

In the USA, parents are actually asked to monitor the games that children play with their friends. When children play violent games or games that glorify antisocial behaviour, they are likely to become prone to such negative behaviour in real life too. And let us not think that such influences are limited to children; think of young men speeding on the highway, racing each other in cars or on bikes; think of a whole group of students 'bunking' class to go to the movies; think of youngsters just driving off to resorts or parties without informing their parents. Such gang or group behaviour spells trouble.

"Let this be the rule of friendship," Cicero tells us, "never to make disgraceful requests, and never to grant them." He adds, rather sadly that men are often more careful about their sheep and goats than about their friends. And he states categorically: "I consider this as a first principle, that friendship can exist only between good men."

In kindergartens and in primary school classes, a responsible teacher sees to it that 'troublemakers' don't sit together and get into double trouble. During teenage years responsible parents tend to keep a watch on the company their children keep. But when we ourselves become responsible adults, it is up to us to choose our friends carefully. And this can help us: not to form attachments too quickly; and to get to know our companions well before we accord them the status of friends.

I can almost hear some of my young friends exclaiming: "But Dada, that's so negative! Our parents are always telling us this, and we would like to tell them to trust our judgment! And parents and teachers must also be told that they must not always look on our friends with suspicion!"

May I say to you, neither your parents, nor your teachers wish to interfere in your friendships! They cannot make your decisions for you, any more than they can eat your food when you are hungry. I also believe that if you pick up a few bad traits or habits from friends, it is also an important part of your growing up – provided you know where to stop! But learning to build healthy friendships is also something important that you should learn; it is part of the process of learning who you are and what is good for you. If your parents do express concern, and deliver a few warnings, take it in your stride and realise that they mean it for your own good!

And to the parents of my young friends, let me say: trust your children; have faith in them and respect their sense of self and their identity. Extend your hand of love and friendship to your children's friends, and make them feel welcome in your home!

We saw earlier that Francis Bacon spoke rather disparagingly of people who chose solitude over company; George Washington on the other hand, said, "It is better to be alone than in bad company."

In the famous play, *A Man for All Seasons* which is about the life and death by execution of Sir Thomas Moore, the chancellor, Sir Thomas is urged by his friends and close companions to support the unfair, unjust diktats of King Henry VIII. "Why can't you do as I did and come with us, for fellowship!" appeals an aristocrat and a friend, the Duke of Norfolk.

Sir Thomas's reply is significant. "And when we die, and you are sent to heaven for doing your conscience, and I am sent to hell for not doing mine, will you come with me, for fellowship?"

If you run with the wolves, you learn to howl, ancient wisdom tells us; and if you fly with the eagles, you learn to soar high in the sky. We all know this from personal experience: we feel drained and depressed in the company of negative people. Positive thinkers will inspire you to achieve greater goals.

A friend shared this thought with me once: that each one of us is actually a compilation of the five people with whom we interact the most. A good friend can teach you a lot that is valuable; a good friend can help you evolve into a better human being; we can learn generosity and acquire wisdom from our friends; and the best way to find such friends is to be, or become such a good friend yourself!

Exercise:

Spend a little time reflecting on the following groups of people in your life:

childhood friends /online friends	boyfriends / girlfriends
long-lost friends	best friends "just good" friends
former friends	school friends/old friends

How many of them are still in touch with you? How often do you communicate meaningfully with them?

What have they contributed towards making you what you are?

Why are friendships important for you? Do you still maintain friendships from the past?

How long have you known your best friend?

Where did you meet and what did you have in common?

Friends Forever

Chapter 3

Why Do We Need Friends?

"I Knew You Would Come!"

Horror gripped the heart of a World War-I soldier, as he saw his lifelong friend hit by the enemy's bullet and fall to the ground in the frontline of the battle.

The soldier requested permission from his captain to go forward and bring his fallen comrade back. "Well, you may go," said the captain. "But do you think it would be worthwhile? Your friend is probably dead by the looks of it, and you may throw your life away."

But the soldier was insistent, and went forward to where his friend lay. Miraculously, he managed to reach his friend, hoisted him onto his shoulder and brought him back to their company's trench. The officer checked the wounded soldier, and saw that he was dead. He looked compassionately at his friend and said to him, in kindness rather than remonstrance, "I told you it wouldn't be worth it."

"It was worth it, Sir," said the soldier.

"What do you mean by worth it?" responded the captain. "Your friend is dead."

"Yes Sir," the soldier answered, "but it was worth it because when I got to him, he was still alive and I had the satisfaction of hearing him say... 'Man...I knew you would come!'"

A true friend is the best possession.
Benjamin Franklin

W hat is it that we want more than anything else?

Chances are that not many of us will answer this question with the single word "Friendship". Human nature being what it is, we crave riches, we crave power, we desire for fame and popularity, positions of honour, sound health and a long life Granted, these things are indeed desirable in life. But these are matters that are beyond our control, and depend on the caprices of fortune or 'luck' as we call it. And then, we all know that today's billionaire might become tomorrow's pauper, given the caprices of the business environment.

Wisdom and virtue are perhaps the greatest gifts that God can bestow on us. But the one thing that we can earn and keep for a lifetime is friendship with good people. For what is pleasure and wealth, if we cannot share it with those who rejoice in our good fortune? And how could we bear our sorrows and miseries if we had no friends to share them and thus have the burden? Thus we have the ancient Latin poet telling us:

> How can life be worth living, if devoid
>
> Of the calm trust reposed by friend in friend?
>
> What sweeter joy than in the kindred soul,
>
> Whose converse differs not from self-communion?

One can of course, live without close friends; but I can't help thinking that life would be so much more meaningful and richer, in every sense of the word, if one were blessed with good friends.

In A Lighter Vein

Are Women biologically 'hardwired' for friendship?

Move over "fight-or-flight", there's a new paradigm in town, the first new model to describe people's stress response patterns in more than 60 years.

The model, called "tend-and-befriend" by its developers, won't replace fight-or-flight. Rather, it adds another dimension to the stress-response arsenal, says University of California, Los Angeles, psychologist Shelley Taylor, PhD, who, along with five colleagues, developed the model.

In particular, they propose that females respond to stressful situations by protecting themselves and their young through nurturing behaviours, the "tend" part of the model, and forming alliances with a larger social group, particularly among women, the "befriend" part of the model. Males, in contrast, show less of a tendency toward tending and befriending, sticking more to the fight-or-flight response, they suggest.

The tend-and-befriend model fills what Taylor sees as a huge gap in the stress response literature: namely, that almost all the studies have been conducted in males and so, therefore, upheld fight-or-flight as the main response to stress.

The tend-and-befriend response, in contrast, fits better the way females respond to stress. It builds on the brain's attachment/caregiving system, which counteracts the metabolic activity associated with the traditional fight-or-flight stress response, increased heart rate, blood pressure and cortisol levels and leads to nurturing and affiliative behaviour.

As for the idea of "befriending" when stressed, Taylor and her colleagues detail evidence from studies in humans that when they are stressed, females prefer being with others, especially other females, while males don't. Indeed, in humans, women are much more likely than men to seek out and use social support in all types of stressful situations, including over health-related concerns, relationship problems and work-related conflicts.

"It is one of the most robust gender differences in adult human behavior," writes Taylor and her colleagues.

In fact, tend-and-befriend may be just as adaptive for men as for women in certain contexts, says Collins, whose research finds no gender differences when examining how often husbands and wives seek support from their most intimate companions, for example, each other.

Monitor on Psychology, American Psychological Association

But to return to our question: why do we need friends? What is the role that friends play in our lives?

Author Carlin Flora has written a book called *Friendfluence*. In it, she outlines the multiple aspects of the very beneficial influence that friends exercise on our lives:

Friends Forever

1. They bring real happiness into our lives.

2. They play a major role in determining our sense of 'self' and give us self-worth and self-dignity.

3. By helping us to know ourselves better, friends contribute to our life-skills; they inspire us to reach our goals, help us cope with problems and enable us to live longer and healthier lives.

4. In school, friendships enhance our learning process; teenage friendships hone our social skills.

5. "Birds of a feather flock together" is a cliché that is broken when we cultivate friends whose interests are different from ours; from dissimilar friends, we learn new things, acquire new interests. Such friends broaden our horizons and add a fresh hue to our lives.

6. Good friendship is self-propagating. Friends help you acquire more friends. The larger our friends' circle, the richer our lives! Of course, some friends will always remain special, but having a large group of friends adds value to living.

7. Being friendly, helpful and supportive are excellent qualities that friends nurture in us.

8. Loneliness, depression and insecurity are unhealthy and harmful tendencies that can come upon us at any time in our lives. Friends are the best antidotes to these joy-killer feelings.

9. Friends help you to be grounded and realistic, by keeping a reality check on you. Many of us tend to get carried away by unrealistic goals and ambitions. A friend who knows us well can hold us back from disastrous flights of fancy.

10. All of us have the aspiration to make this world a better place, at least in our own small way. Friends can help you bring about this change for the better, for as a team or a group, we can achieve much more! Whether it is standing up for a cause we believe in, fighting against a social evil or just raising funds for charity, friends offer us invaluable help and support.

"Being a friend is a great honour and responsibility, so treat your friends carefully," Ms.Carlin tells us. Offering and receiving the great gift of friendship is one of the greatest joys of a well-lived life. Our friends need us, even as we need them. The effort we put in to make friends and keep them will surely make our lives rewarding and fulfilling.

Exercise:

Check out the following in relation to your true friends:

1. Do you both have static roles? (It is one who does most of the talking while the other always listens) Or do you both switch roles? (Sometimes, it is you who call her up; sometimes, she calls you up; sometimes, it is you who are at the receiving end of advice/scolding; sometimes it is her, and so on)

2. Do you both share a give-and-take relationship? Or is it one person who is constantly giving (advice, support, help, confidence and strength) while the other is simply there for a takeaway?

Chapter 4

How to Recognise a
True Friend

For my Best Friend

Tom and Jack lived in Boston. They were not just colleagues, but also neighbours and the best of friends since childhood and virtually inseparable from one another. Tragedy struck their lives when they were driving to a nearby city in connection with their work. The car they were travelling in met with an accident, and both men were severely injured.

The next morning, when Jack came to consciousness, he was in a Boston hospital. He could move his limbs; he could think clearly; he actually felt hungry. But there was a tight bandage around his eyes. The doctor who was attending on him told him that he had lost vision in both his eyes.

Jack was upset. But he asked the doctor, "What about my buddy, Tom?"

Dr. Berkley's voice was grim as he replied, "Tom is still unconscious. He has sustained multiple injuries and will not be able to walk or move his limbs. We are waiting for him to come out of coma."

Jack was discharged from the hospital within a week and he considered himself lucky. His company found him a job which he could handle in the packing department. Gradually life returned to normal.

Tom was not so lucky. When he recovered consciousness, he was told that he would be confined to bed for the rest of his life as a quadriplegic. He too asked after his friend, Jack, and was grieved to hear that Jack had become blind.

For a few weeks, Jack came to visit him regularly in Hospital. His visits always cheered Tom and made him forget his pain and misery. Dr. Berkley would remark in all earnestness that Jack's company did Tom more good than all the treatment he received.

It was a few months before Tom returned home. It was a very lonely life for him now. Jack's visits were all he had to look forward to.

But Jack did not want to spend time with Tom any more. His visits gradually decreased. He said to his family that he felt discouraged and embarrassed to spend time with a severely disabled person like Tom. Soon, he moved out of the locality and found a new place to live.

Tom was depressed and deeply unhappy. He had been so close to Jack, spending all his time in Jack's company that he hadn't really made other friends. His mother and father did their best to keep him in good spirits, but he missed Jack terribly.

The grief and misery finally took their toll. Tom fell seriously ill with kidney failure and was readmitted to hospital. In his last moments of consciousness, he asked to speak to Dr. Berkley...

Shortly afterwards, Tom passed away.

Jack was called to come and see Tom in hospital, but he arrived too late. Dr Berkley gave him a letter and said quietly, "This is for you Jack. Tom asked me to give it to you when he was gone."

Jack handed the letter back to Dr. Berkley and asked him to read it aloud. The letter said, "Dear Jack, I have asked Dr. Berkley to ensure that my corneas are transplanted in your eyes. I have nothing left to live for, but I am happy that you will continue to see this world through my eyes. You have always been my best friend, and this is my dying gift to you."

Dr. Berkley said to Jack, "He asked me to write this letter on the day he learnt that you had lost your vision. He made me promise that I would not tell you about it as long as he was alive. We both knew that he would not live long."

Jack stood still as tears of regret and guilt flowed freely from his eyes.

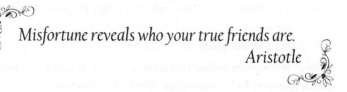

Misfortune reveals who your true friends are.
Aristotle

How to Recognise a True Frien

We have been looking at the reasons why people value friendship and we saw that good and true friends bring us many benefits, even though they are loved selflessly, for their own sake and not for their utility value. We also saw that researchers have affirmed that good health, well-being and a long and contented life are also the fruits of true friendship. We can therefore conclude, that friendship is good for us and essential to our happiness.

But what constitutes 'good' friendship? What are the qualities that distinguish true friends? How can we recognise our true friends?

For many of us, friends appear and disappear at various stages of our life. Not all friendships are lasting. Their company was pleasant while we enjoyed it, but they leave without a trace and we wonder whether they were really our friends.

It is not words and promises, conversations and good fun that mark our true friends. It is their attitude, their actions that reveal their true nature. It was indeed, a wise man who said that a real friend is the one who walks in when the rest of the world walks out.

In a Lighter Vein

Three friends who went deep sea fishing were marooned on a deserted island. They found a magic lantern on the beach and rubbed it hopefully. Sure enough, a genie appeared instantly and said to them: "I shall grant exactly one wish for each of you." Turning to the first man he asked, "What can I do for you?"

"I want to be out of this place and back in my home!" said the first man in great excitement.

And he was gone in an instant.

"And what would you like me to do?" the genie asked the second man.

"I'd like to be back home too!" stammered the second man.

He too, vanished in an instant.

"How about you?" said the genie to the third man.

He scratched his head thoughtfully and pondered a while. Then he brightened and said, "It's going to be so dreadful here without my friends. Please bring them right back!"

Friends Forever

Here are some questions put together by experts to help you determine how true and genuine your friends are:

1. Have they always supported you in your decisions and in moments of crisis?
2. Have they refrained from passing judgments on you?
3. Have they deliberately put you down or mocked you in public?
4. Have they hurt your feelings deliberately and knowingly?
5. Have they always shown kindness and consideration to you?
6. Have they treated you with affection and respect at all times?
7. Have you always felt at ease in their company and found it enjoyable and pleasant?
8. Have they proved that they are loyal and trustworthy?
9. Have they respected your confidence and kept all your secrets?
10. Have they stuck by your side when you were in trouble?
11. Have they always listened to you in patience and sympathy?
12. Have they laughed with you when you were happy and shed tears with you in your sorrow?

If your answer has been yes to most of the questions asked above, let me congratulate you, for you are indeed blessed with true friends.

From the above, it is easy to infer or derive the qualities of a true friend:

1. A good friend listens to you with patience and empathy. This does not mean that he has all the answers to your questions or spot-solutions to all your problems. But he understands you and sees the situation from your point of view. This is not always easy! More often than not, we are ready to offer expert advice and suggestions, before we attempt to understand the other person's point of view. Let us remember this: people, who wish to open up to us, are not always looking for solutions to their problems; sometimes, all they need is a shoulder to lean on, an understanding listener. The best thing that a friend can allow you to do is to think aloud, candidly and spontaneously, in his hearing.

2. A friend in need is a friend indeed. A good friend allows you to spell out what you need from him and tries his best to fulfill that need. Above all, it is great for you to know that your friend is always there for you.

3. Friends stay in touch. They communicate with each other even when they are divided by continents. I don't think this important aspect should be ignored or taken for granted. You cannot take your friend for granted and stay incommunicado. Imagine, if you urgently needed something from him and you call him up after months of silence, wouldn't he feel that you call him only when you want a favour?

4. Friends express their affection, love, regard and appreciation for each other. It is important to let friends know how much they matter to you, by gestures, words and actions. Friendship is not abstract; and our friends need our reassurance. Expressing your feelings makes a big difference to your friends.

5. When your friends are in trouble, you must be prepared to act, even take tough decisions on their behalf. This might be a serious medical condition, a financial crisis or a legal issue: don't wait for the crisis to blow up in your face before you decide to act. Take the initiative, if your friend is not up to it. This can be difficult, especially if you have to act without their consent: but put their welfare first, and act in their interest.

6. Loyalty and trust are aspects that friends cannot compromise on! A friend's betrayal is the unkindest act for any human being, however he may be treated by the rest of the world.

7. A friend is seen as another self; this is why friends often confide their innermost feelings to each other. In this aspect, women are often unfairly accused of betraying confidences and of being unable to keep secrets confided to them in the strictest secrecy. Friends must remember that secrets confided to them are not for chatting or gossip; they are not meant to be shared with others, even those who are close to you.

8. The term 'fair weather friend' is one of the most shameful epithets to apply to any human being. It implies that we are ready to share good times and good fortune with our friends; but when the situation and circumstances are not favourable, we avoid their company. The best example of such fair weather friends are to be found in Jesus's story of the Prodigal Son. If you remember, they gather around the young man as long as he has money to spend; when his fortune is all spent, they disappear from his side, leaving him to wallow in the pigsty. The moral of that story for us in this context is that we must be the first to be by our friend in times of trouble. We must stand up for them when there is no one to support them. To quote the Kural

once again, "As swiftly as the hand moves to seize a slipping garment, friendship acts to assuage a friend's distress".

9. True friends are steady and consistent friends: they do not 'turn on' their friendship when they require a special favour from you. Their friendliness seems to wax and increase manifold when they approach you for help. And they remain friends only so long as they can get something done for you.

10. True friends may not share all your values or principles; but they must respect your belief in those values. A good friend, for instance, will not force you to smoke or drink or eat non-vegetarian food just to prove your friendship!

11. To continue the same circumstance discussed above, a true friend will not hesitate to dissuade you from habits that are harmful to your health and your wellbeing. Most of us are well aware of the fact when we do something that is morally or ethically wrong; is there someone among your friends who has the courage to tell you that what you are doing is wrong and you must desist from it? In the words of Shakespeare, "Grapple them to thy soul with whoops of steel! For he is a true friend indeed!"

12. A true friend is never jealous or possessive to the extent of blaming you for other relationships or friendships in your life. Jealousy and insecurity, or even wanting to monopolise your time and attention are not healthy signs in a good friendship. Just as true friends give each other time and attention, they must also be prepared to give each other space. Friendship makes life worthwhile; friendship adds zest and flavour to life. Friendship may be the salt of life, or the cream of life; but we cannot live on salt or cream. A good friend realises this and does not try to take over your life or crowd out other aspects of your life.

Can you recognise your friends in the above qualities?

What is more important, do you recognise yourself in them?

Exercise:

There is a saying "To have a good friend, you need to be a good friend".

How do you think can you be (or become) a good friend?

How to Recognise a True Friend

Chapter 5

Become Your Own
Best Friend

Who is Your Best Friend

One day we were sitting at the Lotus feet of our beloved master, Gurudev Sadhu Vaswani, when he placed before us this question, "Tell me, who is your best friend?"

A number of answers were offered. Someone said, "A friend in need is the best friend indeed." Someone else said, "Our best friend is even he who knows our faults and failings, who knows our weaknesses and imperfections and still understands us and loves us." And so it went on. Finally, we turned to Gurudev Sadhu Vaswani, and asked him, "Gurudev, pray tell us who is our best friend?"

And Gurudev Sadhu Vaswani said: "You are your own best friend, even as you are your worst enemy."

The Lord gives us the very same teaching in the Bhagavad Gita. Speaking unto his dear, devoted friend and disciple, Arjuna, Sri Krishna says:

> *Bandhuratmatmanastasya*
>
> *Yenatmaivatmanajitah*
>
> *Anatmanastusatrutve*
>
> *Vartetatmaivasatru-vat*

The man who has conquered himself is his own friend, and the man who has not conquered himself is his own foe, his own worst enemy.

No person, no place, nothing has any power over us, for 'we' are the only thinkers in our mind. When we create peace and balance and harmony in our minds, we will find it in our lives.
Louise Hay, You Can Heal Your Life

Have you heard of best selling author Louise Hay?

Nearly thirty years ago, she wrote a book called You Can Heal Your Life. She made a conscious decision not to give the book to any publisher, but to print and publish it herself. The ideas she espoused in the book, she felt, were not in keeping with the general mood or thinking of the 1980s, an age which encouraged success through aggression and strategy. Instead, she decided to start her own publishing venture so that she could put out her new and fresh ideas to the world at large, without looking outside for commercial support. Thus, was born Hay House, one of the world's leading publishers of self-help books. In 1984, when it was first published, the book climbed to the top of the New York Times Bestseller List. Nearly three decades later, in 2009, when Ms. Hay decided to make a film with the same title, the book got back to the top of the same list; and as Louise Hay remarked with a smile, she became a film star at the age of eighty!

You Can Heal Your Life tells us to value ourselves, love ourselves, be kind to ourselves, understand ourselves and thus become the creators of our own destiny. In other words, the message of the book can be summed up in the context of our own little book as: *Become Your Own Best Friend*!

Too many of us, alas, tend to undervalue, underestimate ourselves. Perhaps some of us are even aware of this sense of low self-esteem, low self-worth in which we hold ourselves. (The old fashioned term 'inferiority complex' has thankfully lost currency these days.) We might be aware of this, but we do nothing about it! Or, what is worse, we tend to blame others for our lack of courage and confidence. We blame parents who were too strict or too disciplinarian; we blame teachers who were too harsh or too strict; we blame childhood companions/siblings/cousins who were far more gifted, far more beautiful/good looking and far more popular than we were at that time. When you set out to blame others, you know it is not difficult to find an object of blame!

It's time to stop shifting the blame and take charge of your own life! Let me repeat what I have said to my friends time and again: You are unique! You are a child of God! There is no one quite like you in all the world! You must therefore learn to respect yourself and love yourself, because you must become your own best friend before you go out to make good friends!

Friends Forever

Lift up the self by the Self

And don't let the self droop down,

For the Self is the self's only friend

And the self is the Self's only foe.

That is just another freewheeling expression of the same idea from the Gita that we quoted above. Unless you love yourself, how can you feel yourself worthy of receiving another's love?

Please note: what I refer to here is not self-love in the sense of ego, arrogance, vanity or a self-centered, self-serving attitude. It is simply a matter of accepting yourself with grace and compassion, accepting your weaknesses and limitations with a positive attitude that you can always improve and change for the better.

Forty years ago, a psychiatrist couple, Mildred Newman and Bernard Berkowitz wrote a book which bears more or less the same title as this chapter. Titled How to be Your Own Best Friend, this book too sold over three million copies and touched the lives of many people. What this book stressed more than anything else, was the idea that we have the power and the innate ability to make our own choices and to make ourselves as happy as we choose to be.

Some of you might be forgiven for wondering why Dada is referring to books written thirty or forty years ago! (In fact, we began with Aristotle who lived 2500 years ago, followed by Cicero who followed just five hundred years later.) True, these were books that generated a lot of interest and read avidly in those days when all of us had the leisure to read, reflect and act upon the ideas that they expressed. But I also feel very strongly that these books reflect timeless wisdom which is both sound common sense and the best of ancient thought. Of course, the wisdom of Aristotle, Cicero and Bacon are packaged differently now, so as to be accessible to a generation that is familiar with counseling, self-help and psychiatric support. But the gist, the essence of that 'timeless wisdom' remains the same.

Why can't we be our own best friends?

With many young people, low self-esteem and lack of self-worth is based purely on looks and external appearances.

At a question-answer-session with young people, someone sent a chit to me asking the following question: "Can you please explain why I feel inferior and insecure when I am with people who are tall, fair and intelligent?"

Sri Krishna was not fair! Mahatma Gandhi was not tall! That did not stop them from having a great self-image and an excellent sense of humour.

I cannot understand why young people today aspire to look like film stars, models and sportspersons. How boring the world would be if we all looked like clones of each other, all of us 5'8", all of us fair, and all of us with identical sharp features!

You will not believe how unhappy people become, just because they don't like the way they look. Dark complexioned people wish to be fair; fair-skinned women wish they had less oily skin; men wish to be taller and more muscular; girls wish to be slimmer; boys wish to be smarter…

Why can't you like yourself as you are? Why do you make yourself unhappy over how you look, how you talk, how you walk and how you carry yourself? Who sets the standards by which you judge yourself?

Psychologists tell us that the basic reason for several 'complexes' and negative feelings is the fact that people are not happy with who they are and what they are. They are not ready to accept themselves as they are, they don't like themselves. This leads to low self-esteem, insecurity and negative self-image.

Forensic experts tell us that no two human beings will have similar or identical fingerprints; each one is unique. Now, generic scientists are telling us that our DNA is equally unique. God has chosen to make each one of us uniquely different. Why then should we wish to become copycats? Why should we wish to imitate others and make ourselves unhappy in the process?

You don't have to be the tallest, smartest or the most intelligent person! You must be at your best; you must do your best and that's what counts.

Whom are we trying to please by bending over backwards to try and be what we are not? If you set great store by what others think of you, you will reduce yourself to being a dull and pale imitation of others!

God has made each of us for a distinctive purpose. He has meant some of us to become great artists; some of us were born to become great dreamers and visionaries; some of us were meant for professions like medicine, engineering, architecture or law.

But there are a vast majority of us who are none of these things. May be God meant us to be good human beings; maybe He wanted us to be the helpers and servers of humanity; maybe He meant us to be kind, loving sons/ daughters/ spouses/ parents. Why should we try to alter His divine plan?

Some of us are blessed with material wealth and riches; some of us are blessed with business acumen; some are gifted with artistic bent and creativity; yet others stand apart with their caring and compassionate attitude; a few of us are efficient and capable administrators; sincerity and devotion mark the efforts of some people; the world needs us all. We can each contribute our own special and unique efforts to make life more meaningful and beautiful. What matters is we recognise the others' contributions and appreciate it. In the words of Rabindranath Tagore:

> There are numerous strings in your lute,
> Let me add my own among them.

All of us, with our individual gifts and skills are like so many strings on God's lute. We will make divine music, when we function together.

The idea behind this song too, is that each of us has our own gifts and attributes, unique and distinct from others. We must learn to recognise our own merits and defects, and work with others to promote goodness and harmony in life.

A realistic perspective

It's funny that we think we'll help ourselves by being hard on ourselves, when most people would never try to help their friends or children that way. Here are the things I had to learn:

You don't have to be perfect. You don't expect your friends to be perfect, do you? You're human, too. Nobody can be perfect. Be realistic in your expectations of yourself.

You don't have to know everything. When you encounter something you don't know, you can see it as a threat, or you can see it as a chance to learn and grow. It's easy to be threatened by things you don't know if you take their existence to mean you're inadequate. But it's impossible to know everything! What's more, if you take the opportunity to learn when you're presented with new things, you make yourself more skilled, more knowledgeable, and more awesome all the time.

You can ask for help. This was a tough one for me I always hated admitting I didn't know something or couldn't do everything myself. That would mean I wasn't perfect! But the reality is, nobody can do everything alone. If you ask for help, people won't think you're weak. Accepting help from people you know is actually a great way to get closer.

Many of us feel lost in the immensity of life. Many of us feel unwanted or insignificant in the workplace. Things seem to happen with or without our contribution. Major events and functions happen where we do not have a role to play. At best we are reduced to the level of bystanders or spectators; at worst, we feel unwanted, useless, redundant. This naturally causes a great deal of unhappiness in our hearts.

Can I give you my simple five-step solution for developing a healthy sense of self-respect?

You must become health conscious, you must be help conscious, you must be hope conscious, you must be love conscious, and you must be faith conscious!

Be health conscious: Therefore, do not abuse your body, do not abuse your system. In Indian philosophy, the physical body is not meant to be neglected or devalued. *Shariram Brahma mandiram:* the body is a temple of Brahman, the Universal Spirit. We neglect it at our own peril! Therefore, eat wisely; exercise regularly; and do not fill your stomach with junk food! Take good care of yourself; for this human life is too precious to be neglected or wasted.

Be help conscious: Become an instrument of God's help and healing in this tear-stained, sorrow-smitten world, where millions upon millions are worse off than you, and look to you for support!

We once asked Gurudev Sadhu Vaswani, "Why are we here?" And he said: "We are here to help others." A similar question was asked by a little child of his mother. He asked her, "Mama! Mama! Why are we here?" And his Mama said: "We are here to help others." But the child was not content with the answer. And he asked, "What are the others here for?" We don't have to persist in this fashion; suffice it to understand that all of us need to be help conscious. We have to go out of our way to try to bring sunshine into the lives of those who are living in dark alleys.

Friends Forever

Let us be hope conscious: and though the proverb tells us that 'hope springs eternal in the human breast' may I say to you, we have to create the right conditions in our minds and hearts to let hope flow and flourish.

Scientists tell us that a magnetised piece of steel can lift up iron particles that weigh several times its weight; but if the same piece of steel is demagnetised, it cannot even lift so much as a feather's weight. When you unclutter your mind and cleanse your thoughts, you are magnetising your mind. You will find that confidence, hope and optimism fill your mind and you will achieve success and happiness.

A Samurai maxim tells us: "Control your emotion, or it will control you". I would alter this maxim just a little: Control your negative emotions, or they will control you.

If you wish to be happy, get rid of the joy killers! Gautama Buddha called them "three evils of the mind", lust, hatred and greed. Hatred and happiness can never go together, even as light and darkness can never dwell together! And the Buddha also taught us how to conquer hatred, eliminate it from our lives: "Hatred ceaseth not by hatred; hatred ceaseth by love!"

Which brings us naturally to the next step: be love conscious. But remember, love is for giving, not taking or demanding!

A happily married woman who celebrated her sixtieth wedding anniversary said to a writer who was interviewing her, "Nobody can find love if they go looking for it alone."

Love is not out there somewhere. It is with you, within you. The more you offer love to the world and the people in it, the more it will come back to you! Indeed, it was a wise man who asserted: "Love grows by giving. The love we give away is the only love we keep. The only way to retain love is to give it away".

And last but not the least, be faith conscious: What is faith? Faith is not blind, as some 'rationalists' would claim. Faith is seeing with the eyes of the heart. But alas, with many of us, the eyes of the heart are closed. When we open these eyes, we will see that all that has happened has happened for the best, all that is happening is happening for the best, and all that will happen will happen for the best. There is a meaning of mercy in all that happens. God has a plan for everyone of us, and there is divine purpose in every little thing that happens to us. The great American poet, Whittier, said, "When faith is lost…the man is dead!"

Divine wisdom controls your life. There is a meaning of mercy in everything that happens. And God is infinite love and wisdom: He is too loving to punish us harshly and too wise to make a mistake! This is the quintessence of faith.

Let me repeat the magic remedy to become your best friend: You must become health conscious, you must be help conscious, you must be hope conscious, you must be love conscious and you must be faith conscious!

Exercise:

Here are a few practical suggestions to build your sense of self-worth and help you to become your own best friend:

1. Realise that you are unique, you have been created with certain traits and gifts that are special to you. Because you are not aware of them, it does not mean you are worthless. Try and find out your special strengths and gifts: your friends/teachers/family will only be too happy to point them out for you.

2. Think of what you enjoy doing, singing, dancing, storytelling, drawing, calligraphy, cooking, gardening ... recreate the sense of pleasure and enjoyment that you derive from these activities, and add more such activities to your daily routine.

3. Participate in the social activities of your group, your community and your neighbourhood. Do not allow yourself to become isolated from your neighbours and friends. Connecting with others, participating in such activities draws you out and gives you the awareness that you are part of a cosmic whole.

4. Give more meaning to your life by finding a worthy cause to which you can devote your energies, it may be an NGO, a *satsang,* a social service group or anything you believe in.

5. Learn to be kind to yourself! Do not criticise yourself or call yourself names constantly! Take good care of yourself physically and mentally.

6. Avoid the company of people who put you down constantly. Do not allow others' criticism to affect your self-image.

7. Make a difference to others, and you will see what a difference it makes in your attitude and personal life! Therefore, go out of your way to help others and make life better for them.

8. Above all, always remember that God loves you and created you to fulfil His special purpose. When you know that He loves you and trusts you, how can you think poorly of yourself?

Section II

HOW TO MAKE GOOD FRIENDS AND KEEP THEM

PRACTICAL SUGGESTIONS

Practical Suggestion 1

Permit Your Friends to be Themselves

Putting Frienship First

I wonder if you have heard of EVR Periyar, an opinion leader and social reformer who played a tremendously influential role in the politics of Tamil Nadu, although he himself never occupied any public office. He was a rationalist who fought aggressively against casteism, superstitions and suppression of women. The term "Periyar" actually means "great leader" in Tamil; and Shri EVR was the only person on whom this title has been bestowed; in fact he is referred to by this title, rather than by his own name.

It is a well-known fact that Periyar was also, among other things, a strong and aggressive atheist. His atheism at times even took an offensive turn, causing him to be caught in controversies. But Periyar counted among his friends several leaders who were pious Hindus and believers, one of whom was Sir. C. Rajagopalachari, fondly referred to as Rajaji. Rajaji was not only a Governor-General of independent India; he also became the Chief Minister of Chennai state in a hard-fought election in which Periyar's supporters tried their best to defeat him. They continued to keep up their bitter attacks even after he became chief minister. But during all these days, the old friendship between Periyar and Rajaji stayed firm and steady.

Rajaji was also a writer of repute who translated the Ramayana, the Mahabharata and the Gita into Tamil. His commentary on the Upanishads is also highly acclaimed. That a staunch believer and a committed atheist should remain lifelong friends is a measure of the strength of their respective personalities. Here is a little-known eye witness account of one of their meetings.

Once, Periyar fell seriously ill. Concerned for his health, Rajaji visited him at home, and when the friends had greeted each other warmly, Rajaji applied on Periyar's forehead, the sacred *vibhuti*, *kumkum* which he had brought from a special *pooja* he had performed at a temple for his friend. Periyar accepted this gesture with gratitude; the two friends discussed politics and the state of the country. Rajaji left after a while.

Permit your friends to be themselves.

One of Periyar's friends who was present at the meeting fumed at Rajaji's audacity in applying *vibhuti* on Periyar's forehead. "You should have rubbed it off then and there, sir, to show him where you stand," he said angrily.

"Why should I do that?" countered the leader. Rajaji is a dear friend; and the *prasad* he brought from the temple was a token of his regard and concern for me. It is a symbol of our friendship. What does our friendship have to do with the fact that he is a believer and I am a non-believer?"

A true friend is even he who knows my faults and failings, my weaknesses and my imperfections, my limitations and my lapses, and still loves me.

Sadhu Vaswani

A teenager once said to me in despair, "I wonder why people become your friends and then try to change everything about you. Surely my friend knew me well and knew what type of a person I was, before she became friends with me. One assumes that if you become friends with someone you are friends with them for who they are, and not for some imaginary version of who you want them to be!"

The two girls in question had been friends throughout school; Leena was a quiet and serious girl while Mona was spirited and fun loving. Their widely different personalities had only cemented their friendship, for Leena saw to it that her friend's exuberant spirits did not get her into trouble; while Mona made sure that her sober friend was always involved in those 'fun' times that make our schooldays so memorable.

The trouble started when the friends joined college. I am afraid that getting into college goes directly 'to the heads' of some youngsters! They see college not just as having freedom and feeling 'grown up'; they take their sense of liberation so far that they think it nothing to break a few rules, bunk lectures and otherwise showing themselves as 'free' spirits who cannot be curbed by discipline. Mona was determined to have fun all the time. She constantly pressurised Leena to join her in her escapades to coffee shops and movies during class hours; this, the timid Leena absolutely refused to do. In fact, she urged Mona to change her ways, lest she should get into trouble. But Mona was determined to 'have fun' at all costs. She began cutting her classes, and when she was pulled up for shortfall in attendance, she pressurised Leena into giving 'proxy' attendance for her. Horrified by the very suggestion, Leena refused her friend's request outright. Mona was not angry or upset. But she began a sustained attempt to 'change' her friend; and she chose subtle arguments to assist her brainwashing programme. "We are only young once… these years will never come back to us… college is not like school… we are adults now, we can vote… shouldn't we just forget everything else and have fun?"

Quiet and timid she might be, but Leena was also a girl who knew her own mind. She pointed out to Mona that having fun at the expense of lectures was not her idea of college life. And as for giving proxy attendance, it was out of the question!

For many of us, this might seem an adolescent problem. But this is only an example to show you that a certain level of acceptance is necessary in good friendship.

There is a caveat I must add here: you MUST try and change your friends if they are destroying themselves by their bad habits! If your friend is a chain smoker or

Permit your friends to be themselves.

excessive coffee drinker or drives his bike too fast it is your moral obligation to break that bad habit and change him for the better! If your friend is overweight, it is your duty to help her take up a diet/exercise/fitness regime that will help her become fit and healthy. If your friend is indulging in anti-social activities or breaking the laws, you must try and stop him! And no, I am not contradicting myself by introducing this caveat. As a friend, it is your sacred obligation to tell your friend that he is doing something wrong and to try to get him to break the habit that is potentially harmful to his well-being.

What do I mean when I say that you should accept your friends as they are? I mean simply, that you must not try to change their personalities to suit your tastes and lifestyle. You must not try to make your friend your clone!

Many of us consciously choose friends who share our interests, attitudes and hobbies. Equally, many of us are drawn towards friends who are not in the least like us in temperament and interests. If you are a stressed, highly strung individual, you will surely love a friend who can make you laugh and help you relax! If you are in a high-pressure job, you may love to spend time in the company of a friend who discusses all the books he has read with you. If you are a full time teacher, you may enjoy spending time with a neighbour who is a fulltime homemaker, wife and mother.

Some people are happy if they have friends who are like them in every way. They feel that if they are of the same nature and share the same interests, they can understand each other's feelings better; go out to share common activities like walking, trekking, visiting museums or attending music concerts. They like to talk about issues of common interest, and here too, their discussions are friendly and easy, because they share the same opinions. This, they feel, makes for long-standing friendship.

I see their point: but I also see the pitfalls! If people should have the same interests, same opinions and even speak the same language for good friendship, how limited our friends' circle would be! I have actually heard people say, "If two people talk in different languages, then they cannot be good friends. For friendly communication, language is very important. I always prefer those friends who speak with me in my mother tongue."

But very many people are happy to have friends who are not at all similar to them. They feel that such friends give them exposure to aspects of life which they know nothing of! They talk about a wide variety of subjects, gracefully agreeing to disagree when they have differing points of view.

One of the things I admire most in politicians whose friendships cut across narrow party lines. I am afraid this is becoming increasingly rare these days. But in the good old days, it was not at all an uncommon sight to see bitter political rivals emerging out from heated parliament sessions, laughing and chatting together. This is not just civility and good etiquette but also the personal ability to keep politics and personal lives apart. Further, it promotes greater understanding and tolerance in society as a whole.

Equally sensitive is the friendship between extroverts and introverts; if you are the party-hopping type who cannot bear to be alone at home, don't drag your bookworm friend to join you! Once you have dragged her there, you will insist that she joins the fun, you will insist that she indulges in chitchat and gossip which she might detest and you might force her to stay up late and return home at what she considers to be unacceptably late hours!

Don't Assume that your friend is like you and enjoys everything that you do! A friend sent me this funny statement about assume: When you assume anything, you make an Ass out of U and ME! This is especially important when you and your friend do not share the same faith and the same political opinions.

Live and let live! This is tolerance at its best. Why should I expect my friend to think and work and speak and worship as I do? Let me accept that all of us are different and let me respect the difference. For all our differences, for all our diversity in language, culture and religion, we share but one world. Therefore, let us accept differences nay, celebrate all differences, and take delight in them! In difference is variety, the spice of life. In diversity is strength.

In India, we celebrate the plurality and multiplicity of our languages and cultures. The poet Subramanya Bharati described Mother India as the glorious lady who spoke eighteen different languages and had 30 million different faces to show. My friends, that was nearly a hundred years ago. Our population was then just thirty million, and the British recognised only eighteen Indian languages. Today, we are a nation of a billion people, and experts say our people speak over two hundred dialects! In this amazing collection of over a billion people, why should you restrict your friendship to those who speak your language or come from the same region as you do?

I strongly believe that a peace plan for this strife torn age must necessarily start as a friendship plan at the individual level. Therefore, we must go out and make friends

Permit your friends to be themselves.

with people belonging to different religions, different communities and nationalities. This is what friendship is all about; not just sticking to the people you know, your neighbours, your colleagues, the people you grew up with.

It is a trite commonplace today to say that the world has become a global village. In my own city of Pune, we have students from Iran, Iraq, Nigeria and Thailand seated side by side with Indian youngsters at the University. As for the USA, young people from all over the world congregate in the universities. Now more than ever, global friendships can become a reality!

Exercise:

Write down the names of a dozen of your good friends.

Against each name put down their age, their social background, their profession, their community and their language. Note down too, their political leanings and their special interests.

What is the pattern that emerges? Are you consciously associating with those who share your views and your background? Or does your friendship cut across narrow barriers of language, region and community?

Practical Suggestion 2

Be Honest with your Friends: Express your true Feelings

Maricha's Honest Opinion

Most of us who claim to be familiar with the Ramayana, think of Maricha as the evil demon who took on the form of the golden deer to lure Sri Rama away from Sita, as Ravana's evil minded friend and supporter. A closer reading of the Aranya Kanda will show that this was not quite the case!

Maricha was an *asura*, the son of Thataka, the cruel and bloodthirsty demoness killed by the sixteen year-old prince Rama, to protect Sage Vishwamitra's *yajna*. In the fierce battle at Tatakavana, she and her younger son, Subahu were both destroyed; however, her elder son Maricha was thrown hundreds of leagues away by Rama's arrow, and managed to survive.

Chastened by the divine encounter, Maricha chose to live a life of repentance and meditation in a remote forest. It was here that Ravana came to meet him when the deadly notion of capturing Sita came to him. He felt that it was only Maricha who could help him with this evil scheme, and appealed to him for help.

Maricha was not just appalled by the scheme, but had the courage and honesty to tell Ravana that he was seeking his own doom and the destruction of his clan. He described in detail Rama's valour and integrity and above all his adherence to *dharma*. "Do not take on yourself the sin of opposing Rama who is the very personification of *dharma*," he warned Ravana. "It is a terrible sin to covet another man's wife. And Rama is no ordinary mortal. This scheme of yours will only spell doom and destruction for all of us!"

According to Valmiki Ramayana, Ravana accepts Maricha's good counsel and returns to Lanka. Unfortunately, Surpanaka's evil counsel makes him turn to his evil design once again. This time, he threatens Maricha with death unless he cooperates with him. Deeply saddened, Maricha agrees to help him, prophesying the catastrophe to follow, and choosing death at Sri Rama's hands as a means of his own salvation.

Had Ravana listened to Maricha's good counsel and honest warning, things might have been very different for him!

Some people will not tolerate emotional honesty in communication. They would rather defend their dishonesty on the grounds that it might hurt others. Therefore, having rationalised their phoniness into nobility, they settle for superficial relationships.

Author Unknown

Be honest with your friends: Express your true feelings.

We all want friends whom we can trust. Honesty is the basis of all trust. If you want to be a true friend, you cannot afford to be less than honest with your friends! If you are looking for friends who will constantly flatter you and tell you only what you want to hear, you are looking for yes-men, not friends. One of the reasons why we value our good friends is because we know they will "tell it to us like it is" to quote the popular expression; or "give it to us straight" as we say.

We all know the famous statement, "Honesty is the best policy". It sounds so simple and easy, doesn't it? But it's not so easy to practise it in thought, word and deed. Psychologists tell us that we take to dishonesty as children, when we realise that certain words or utterances produce outcomes that are favourable to us. Especially crucial is the realisation that saying something ("I promise to do my homework right away") or not saying something ("Who broke this jar?" "….") gets us a favourable response; we begin to slip easily into dishonesty without a second thought. This attitude becomes so entrenched in our subconscious that we begin to utter falsehoods without even realising that we are uttering lies! If this goes on repeatedly, we actually lose the moral sensitivity to realise where truth ends and dishonesty takes over.

"Whoever is careless with the truth in small matters cannot be trusted with important matters," said Einstein. If our friends start thinking this about us, there's an end to understanding and trust!

But at the same time, people often ask: "Can you be absolutely honest and still keep your friends?" Being honest, they feel, might only hurt their friends and cost the relationship dear. Who likes or wants to be told bitter, unpleasant truths? And which is more important in friendship, honesty or kindness?

Consider the following questions (purely imaginary) that your best friend may put to you:

1. Does this dress look good on me? (This, when the girl in question is wearing a totally unsuitable outfit which does not in the least flatter her appearance.)

2. Wasn't I smart? Gave it back to him didn't I? (This, when the young man has been rude and offensive to the teacher and has been thrown out of class.)

3. You will always support me, won't you? (This, when your friend is

indulging in antisocial or criminal behaviour.)

4.   Do you think I've put on weight? (This, from a friend who has a medical condition and has been warned to keep her weight under control.)

All of us know we can respond in ways that do not hurt our friends' feelings and, for many of us, that is of paramount importance.

Take the first question: your friend might actually be making a sad spectacle of herself at a party or gathering where people might be laughing or making fun of her. To tell her that she is looking fine or that the dress looks good on her is hypocrisy and dishonesty. You can tell her in gentle terms what someone else will tell her very harshly: "My God! Where did you get that outfit? It makes you look twenty kilos heavier and ten years older!"

As for the second, it is important to make your friend understand that being rude to a teacher is not exactly your idea of being smart. Such foolish attempts at bravado, when supported by mindless friends, can turn an ordinary young man into a goon!

A friend indulging in antisocial behaviour might seem very remote to many of you at this point in time. But of late we have been reading horrendous news reports of schoolboys who kidnap their friends for ransom and kill them out of fear! I am sure it all started as a lark, a bit of harmless fun! Draw the line at such foolish ventures. Tell your friend that such ideas are not brave or trendy; they are bad and might lead you into lifelong trouble!

I am deeply saddened to hear young people in a group who mindlessly cross the line between fun-loving and trouble-making behaviour.

Five years ago, a group of youngsters returning from a party in Chennai, decided to give chase to a girl on a scooter. They rammed into her two-wheeler, forcing her to veer to the right where she hit a road barrier and was killed on the spot. All the five were booked for manslaughter. If only one of the boys had said to his friends, "Enough is enough! Let's leave the girl alone."

Every year in Pune, the police raid New Year parties being held at resorts and vacant farmhouses. Over a hundred young people (boys and girls), most of them students from good colleges are caught with drugs. Surely someone started it off by saying "Let's have some fun!" and nobody among the group had the honesty and the guts to say, "This is not fun; it's illegal!"

It is perfectly possible for us to be honest without being brutal or hurtful; sometimes our friends ask us for an honest opinion; sometimes we ourselves need

Be honest with your friends: Express your true feelings.

to speak up and tell them what we think is good for them. In either case, if we are valued as true friends, then it is to us that our friends will turn when they need to know the truth. You can be honest without being brutal; you can give them the truth without insulting them or putting them down as worthless. Tact is not equal to untruth. And a timely warning is not unsolicited advice. It is your loving concern expressed with honesty.

You and your friend are taking a joyride in his new car. He begins to drive a little recklessly. You should tell him straightaway, "Slow down! We want to get back in one piece, don't we?"

Your friend is making yet another attempt at the UPSC examination. He has failed thrice; you know he is not of the caliber to make it; rather than pushing him to take on what is clearly beyond him, you should have the honesty to tell him to give up the frustrating effort and try something else instead. One day, he will thank you for it!

Most sensible people, young or old, are not looking for yes-men or hangers-on or mere sycophants when they look for friends! The former can be bought or hired; friends, honest, truthful, trustworthy ones are not so easy to find. And when sensible friends seek your opinion, they don't just want your agreement, they want the truth. False appreciation and hypocrisy will only make you lose respect in your friends' eyes. Honesty will strengthen your friendship and build up your sense of mutual respect.

Thus far, we have spoken of giving your friends an honest opinion: the other side of the coin is being honest about your feelings, your problems and your experiences with your friends. Many of us are very reluctant to 'share' our secrets with friends, beyond a certain point. Of course, it is entirely up to you how much of your life you really wish to share with friends. But it is wonderful to have friends (beyond the family circle) with whom we can open up and be ourselves! For this, we have to kindle and nurture a sense of trust and loyalty. Totally honest communication is possible only in a relationship of trust. When this is achieved, friendship can offer healing, help and comfort to wounded sensibilities and aching hearts. But this must come naturally; it must evolve out of well-founded loyalty and regard.

When a friend opens up to you, be sure to listen with empathy and understanding. Reserve your judgment and criticism for later. Afford your friend the opportunity to unburden her heart and find the solace and comfort she needs. Recognise that her honesty to you is a mark of the great affection she holds for you. Respect her confidence and her trust.

Honesty in friendship not only offers timely help and encouragement; it can also be a source of help and healing. Above all else, it strengthens the bonds of friendship and breaks the barriers of isolation and loneliness.

Exercise:

1. Do you listen to your friends patiently when they are trying to tell you something which they find difficult to share?

2. Do you share your innermost feelings and insecurities with trusted friends?

3. When your friend is about to take a wrong decision or make a wrong choice, do you speak up against it? Or do you refrain from 'interfering' with her decision for fear of making it unpleasant between the two of you?

4. Are you honest with your friends at all times, in all matters?

Be honest with your friends: Express your true feelings.

Practical Suggestion 3

Let your Friends have their own Space

Seeing Beyond the Wall

I had breakfast with my friend a year or so ago, and it was at the time I started to analyse decisions I had made and not made around my lifestyle. Passing out from graduate school and then jumping into a job four days later, I forgot to read, write, learn, go to the doctor, breathe, sleep, or perform any necessary task needed to just be. I was sitting with my friend at a cafe, staring in front of us. My friend looked at the brick wall across the street, and asked me what I saw, to which I responded, "Uh... a wall." He responded in his Mr. Miyagi way and said, "No you are constantly seeing past the wall, 100 steps past it, and you cannot just appreciate what it is right in front of you".

It sunk in even deeper when another friend of mine (I have a lot of great friends who tell it to me straight) told me that I was so busy living in this elevated space of wanting to change the world, I couldn't just focus on being present and expressing myself based on present situations. I started to realise I needed space from everyone telling me who I was and where I wanted to be so I could figure it out for myself. I couldn't drop off the face of the earth, I couldn't move to India for months on end and meditate (even though that sounded awesome after four years of throwing myself into New York City like a workhorse), but I knew I needed to create space for myself to be able to figure out who I was and what I wanted.

I took time to think about what I wanted from life, and when I say life, I do not mean work. I webbed ideas of what I wanted for myself, the people I wanted to be around, prioritise, and how for some instances, wanted to work with. I thought of space as in location, where I needed to be in order to say yes to only the necessary things I needed to say yes to, and say yes to myself more often. I thought of space as in space from people. There were some people I realised were energy suckers who somehow removed themselves from my life, there were others who loved me very much and whom I loved, but who I needed space from to be able to figure out what was best for me. For those who did not understand, I knew they were taking

Let your friends have their own space

up unnecessary space, for those who did, I knew these were the type of people I wanted in my life, supportive, loving and loyal friends who allowed me the space to be me and step into my own life.

Amanda Slavin

Giving people the space for self-confidence is by far the most important thing that I can do for them. Because then they will act.

Jack Welch

"I like to have my space," is an often heard assertion today.

In an increasingly crowded, congested world, people are becoming conscious of the value that is attached to their own space: space here being not just physical space, but their own privacy and freedom to have the opportunity for doing what they want to do without constant demands and interruptions, not just from outsiders, but also from their near and dear ones.

True, we are social animals; but as human beings we value our own space. If we wish to cultivate strong bonds of friendship, we should avoid invading their personal space, which is sacrosanct to everyone! These days, even married couples have learnt to respect each other's privacy and do not take each other for granted. Children in affluent homes are given their own rooms for study as well as leisure activities. In our Mira Institutions, we keep the campus open during working hours during vacations and outside regular class hours, so that students who do not have this privacy and space at home may make use of the library or the reading halls for this purpose.

When you respect people's sense of personal space, you strengthen the bonds of relationship with them.

Close friends are by no means those who live in each other's pockets! Some of my good friends are people whom I meet after long intervals and with whom I can pick up the thread of friendship effortlessly, as if there has been no break or gap after we left off the last time.

Friendship means caring and sharing; friendship means being there for your friends when they need you; but friendship is not being available on demand 24x7! This is unrealistic and crushing and can only sap the spirit of true friendship.

Each of us has to be our own best friend; only then can we hope to become true friends to others. Always being available to others, always willing to listen, always being on call can only lead to resentment and constriction. True, you must give of yourself in all worthwhile relationships. But giving time and space does not mean compromising yourself, or making a martyr out of yourself. After all, you are a person, a living human being; and so is your friend; you need each other as thinking individuals, sensitive persons, not as doormats or table objects! If you and your friend wish to evolve, grow spiritually and become better individuals, PQT (Personal Quiet Time) is indispensable for both of you!

Let your friends have their own space

Most of the time we tend to focus on being there for our friends; ready to help them on call; always willing to lend our ears or offer our support. This is all very well; but occasionally, we must know how to step back, just a little, and allow our friends to be by themselves, or may be even spend some time with others. Friendship cannot flourish on too many rules or demands. You and your friend may be making new friends individually; friendship is not sole possession or proprietary; ensure that you have time and space for them too.

Many people form lasting friends at the workplace. They meet mostly during working hours, but still remain good friends. Sometimes, they avoid calling up or meeting each other after work, deciding to wait till the next day. This is perfectly acceptable. In fact, it is a little excessive if they decide to call each other soon after they return from work!

From a very young age, we are conditioned to think and act and respond in a certain way. Mothers get more and more fussy and (sometimes) more and more possessive; wives think they have the right to invade their husband's privacy anytime they like; children think they can make demands on their mothers all the time; we feel "always being there" for our friends is essential...

There can be too much of a good thing!

I am afraid we live in a world where everyone talks far too much! We talk excessively in public and in private. As a wise man put it, "Men seem to feel the need to cloak and excuse their imperfections and wrong deeds in a mass of prattle." We need to devote a few minutes each day to the healing, soothing, purifying influence of solitude and silence. You require your space as much as your friends do!

It is vital that we cultivate the healing habit of silence in this age of noise and ceaseless activity. In fact, the great need of modern man is silence. To help us to avoid stress and tension, the noted psychologist, Deborah Bright, recommends what she calls PQT, Personal Quiet Time, of twenty minutes, twice a day.

Alas, in the mechanical rush of the modern world, we have lost touch with the cultivation of silence and solitude. Our lives are getting increasingly complicated; the list of things to be done gets longer, while 24 hours seem to get shorter! At the end of the day, we feel drained, exhausted, emotionally and mentally weary. Where can we find retreat from this spiritual exhaustion? The Roman philosopher Marcus Aurelius has the answer: Nowhere can man find a quieter or more untroubled retreat than in his own soul.

It seems to me that many people today are terrified of silence, afraid of being alone. I know several couples who do not like to spend a quiet evening at home, by themselves. They invite friends over, or go over to clubs or to restaurants so that they do not face solitude. I even know a few people in whose homes the TV is always switched on, even when no one is watching it! They tell me it is comforting to hear the sound/noise from the TV!

Why are we afraid of solitude and silence? Possibly because we cannot bear to look deep within ourselves! This is why many people say they don't have time for silence or meditation. But they will realise, when they go deep within themselves, that the Infinite is within, and we have nothing to fear!

When you sit in silence, you create a space within yourself. In that space you can establish your relationship with God. You can do this by creating beauty in that space, the beauty and glow of love.

Discover that space for yourself, and let your friend discover its joys, too!

Exercise:

Discover the pleasures of PQT (Personal Quiet Time)

1. Reserve for yourself at least fifteen minutes of PQT (Personal Quiet Time) during the day to reflect, introspect and talk to yourself on positive living.

2. Rediscover the beautiful habit of reading. Read at least twenty pages of a classic, a great masterpiece or inspirational literature every day. If you decide to turn to the scriptures for daily reading, that would be better than everything else!

3. At least for an hour during the day, switch off your Mobile Phone, put away your i-Pad and stop being a slave of your own scheduling!

4. Do something creative. Rediscover the fine art of hobbies. Sing, dance or paint your heart out!

Let your friends have their own space

Practical Suggestion 4

Always be ready to offer help: A friend in need is a friend indeed!

Damon and Phyntias

Damon and Phyntias lived on the island of Sicily, outside the ancient city of Syracuse. The ruler of Syracuse in those days was one of the most cruel tyrants known in history, King Dionysius. He was intolerant, unjust and brooked no opposition from anyone. His people suffered under the yoke of his tyranny. But no one could stop the cruelties he perpetrated against them.

Phyntias spoke out against the atrocities of the king: tragically, Dionysius heard of his outburst, and the worst came to pass. He ordered Phyntias to be arrested and pronounced the death sentence on him.

Phyntias was a young man of truth and integrity. The prospect of death did not worry him. But he wanted to return to his native village and bid goodbye to his old mother; he also wanted to ensure that she would be well cared for after his death. He therefore, requested the permission of the king to grant him a respite of a few days so that he could make his last visit to her.

The tyrant King laughed outright. "Don't speak to me of a brief respite," he said to Phyntias mockingly. "I know what you would do if I granted you that respite. You would go into hiding and not return to face your execution. No! You will stay in prison until the day of your execution."

At this point, Damon came forward to offer help to his friend. He said to the King, "If you let my friend go and visit his parents, I offer to be lodged in prison in his place, until he returns. I will be your surety against his return."

Dionysius thought for a while. "Your friend is a rogue, and you are a fool," he said to Damon. "Alright. I will let your precious friend go to his village. But he and you had better be warned. If he does not return before the day appointed for his execution, you shall hang in his place!"

Phyntias protested at the very idea. "It is enough that I have become a

Always be ready to offer help: A friend in need is a friend indeed!

victim of his cruelty and injustice," he said to Damon. "I will never leave you to suffer for my misdeeds." But Damon convinced him that he should make that final visit to his old parents. "You will return well before the appointed day," he assured Phyntias. "And my dear friend, should you not return in time, believe me, I shall be happy to die in your place."

Phyntias's protests fell on deaf ears. Damon forced his friend to go and see his mother. Accordingly, Phyntias was granted permission to visit his mother for the last time, while Damon took his place in the prison.

Days passed. There was no news of Phyntias. The day of execution arrived, but Phyntias had failed to report to the jailor. The whole of Sicily was buzzing with the news that a prisoner sentenced to death had been sent out on parole and had failed to return: and his friend was being sent to the gallows by the tyrant King.

Under the barbaric King, executions were conducted at the public amphitheatre, as if such a spectacle would be of entertainment value to the public. On the appointed day, the amphitheatre literally overflowed with people: Dionysius was seated on his throne, with his mocking sneer. There was no sign of Phyntias. Damon walked up to the gallows, unmoved by his dire fate.

"So this is your friend's final gift to you," mocked the tyrant. "You were a fool to offer to step into his shoes! Look where your precious friendship has brought you, to the foot of the gallows. Don't you regret your hasty decision?"

"I have no regrets whatever," Damon replied. "My only fear is that some mishap may have befallen my friend, or else he would surely have been here by now. But I assure you, I am happy to die in his place. I only ask you this: should he happen to return to you after my execution, spare his life. You cannot punish two people for one offence. As you are the King, give me your word of honour before the people."

Dionysius roared out in laughter. "You fool, you fool," he crowed, "Can't you see that your friend has played a dirty trick on you? He will never return to Syracuse as long as he lives. He has made you his scapegoat, and you are pleading for his life. I haven't come across such a pair of friends like you two!"

As the people watched with bated breath, Damon was led to the gallows. The executioner's axe was raised, and ready to fall on his neck, when a disheveled and distraught Phyntias ran into the stadium, crying loudly, "Stop! Stop the execution! My friend must not be killed. I am here to undergo my death sentence."

He rushed to the gallows, and untied the hands of his friend Damon. "Forgive me, forgive me," he begged. "The ship I was sailing in was captured by pirates, who held me prisoner all these days. I managed to escape from their clutches and rushed back here as soon as I could. Dear Damon, walk away from this place, for you are a free man. I embrace my death willingly, nay, joyously, in the happy thought that I have saved you from an unfair death."

"No Phyntias, no," cried Damon. "I am fully prepared to meet my death now. And believe me, I am happy to die in your place. How I wish the pirates had detained you a little longer! I have already obtained your pardon from the King. You must live on, for nothing will make me happier."

And so, before the astonished eyes of the tyrant King, the two friends stood arguing with each other at the foot of the gallows, each one offering to die in the other's place. There was not a dry eye in the crowd, for the people were truly moved by this spectacle of true love, sacrifice and selflessness.

It melted the hard heart of Dionysius, and he forgave both the friends.

Is this not true friendship? But let us admit, such friendship is rare.

Misfortune shows us those who are not really our friends.

Aristotle

Always be ready to offer help: A friend in need is a friend indeed!

D o you remember your schooldays, when most of you would have been asked to write essays on those topics that are a perennial favourite with most English teachers: "My Best Friend" or "A Friend in Need is a Friend Indeed"? How many of our friends have always been there for us when we needed them?

A true friend is one who is with you in rough weather and tough times: he is the one you can always rely on to help you out of difficulties. He is not just there to share the good times with you; he is ever ready to support you in your hour of crisis, ever ready to sacrifice his personal benefits for your sake, when the circumstances require it.

These days, sacrifice and selflessness are not held up as virtues or desirable attributes in friendship. Ours is an age which believes in "Each one for himself" and "Win at all costs". Perhaps, even the idea of laying down your life for a friend might even seem preposterous to some of my readers.

The origin of the phrase "A friend in need is a friend indeed" takes us back to the Latin writer Ennus Quintius belonging to the 3rd Century B.C. who wrote: "A sure friend is known when in difficulty". The point made is of course that we can count on several fair-weather friends to give us the pleasure of their company when the going is good; but it is only true friends who are by our side when we are in need, when we face crises and difficult situations. We had quoted this earlier: "A true friend is one who walks in when the rest of the world walks out on you".

What kind of need? One might be in a financial crisis, in need of money; one might be caught in the toils of law, in need of support; one might have fallen into wrong company, and in need of redemption; in all such situations, a true friend is there by our side, reassuring us that we are not alone. Self-serving friends disappear in such situations. But good friends rush to our rescue.

Let us face this: not all of us are called upon to offer our lives at the altar of friendship as Damon was. But we can always ensure that we are with our friends through thick and thin. Here are a few suggestions in this regard:

1. Assure your friends that you are always there for them. Even if you are not face to face, keep in touch with them so that they know they are not alone.

2. Listen to their problems with patience and sympathy. For many people in trouble, this alone can bring a tremendous sense of relief.

3. Do not play the blame game; do not point a finger at their lack of discretion or judgment; the lessons and warnings can come later; help and support must take precedence.

4. Ensure that you are available for them until the crisis passes. Do not desert them halfway through the problem.

5. Advice, ideas and suggestions alone cannot help in crisis situations. Actions are more important than words.

6. Different people react to difficulties in very different needs; if you are a good friend, you will know what your friend expects from you. It may not always be material help. It may be just moral or emotional support; it may be silent understanding; it may just be your reassuring presence; or it might be some practical action that might help diffuse the crisis. Understand what your friend needs most at the time, and offer it unconditionally.

And most important of all, stay with them in emotional support until the whole crisis has passed.

I remarked in passing that not all of us will be required to lay down our lives for our friends; but I know many of our friends face life-or-death situations these days. I am agonised to read about the growing number of suicides these days, especially among young people. I am convinced that a person chooses suicide as an option only when he feels there is nobody who understands him, nobody to support him or help him. Depression, isolation and a sense of alienation are rampant among the youth today. I can think of no better panacea for all these psychological ailments than the soothing, healing balm that friendship can offer.

If you read self-help medical guides, you will be quite startled by the common symptoms of clinical depression:

- ❖ a depressed mood during most of the day, especially in the morning
- ❖ a sense of fatigue, exhaustion or low energy levels almost every day
- ❖ constant feeling of worthlessness or guilt
- ❖ lack of concentration, inability to take firm decisions
- ❖ excessive sleeping or lack of sleep
- ❖ refusal to take an interest in family/community

Always be ready to offer help: A friend in need is a friend indeed!

- ❖ recurring thoughts of death or suicide
- ❖ a sense of restlessness
- ❖ significant weight loss or gain

Experts say that if you have even five of these symptoms, you might be suffering from severe depression.

A friend who read these symptoms on a website said to me that he was startled to realise that he had most of them, almost every day!

The reason why I have listed out these common symptoms is so that you might learn to be sensitive to what are called "mood swings" or other warning signs in your friends' behaviour and ensure that they do not go to such drastic lengths.

According to the National Institute of Mental Health, USA, it is estimated that, by the year 2020, major depression will be second only to ischemic heart disease in terms of the leading causes of illness in the world. But people with depression sometimes fail to realise (or accept) that there is a cure to their depressed moods. As a result, they may search endlessly for external causes.

In the U.S., about 14.8 million adults suffer from major depression, according to the National Institute of Mental Health. The sad thing is that many of these people actually attempt suicide. Unfortunately, most people with clinical depression never seek treatment. Left undiagnosed and untreated, depression can worsen, lasting for years and causing untold suffering, and possibly suicide.

So you see, a friend can actually help save another's life just by being extra sensitive and understanding!

People who live alone, people fighting major illnesses, people who have been bereaved, people who have suffered sudden financial losses are especially vulnerable. What can we do if our friends are put through such tests? Let us not think that these issues are too big for us to handle. Let us be there for them, offer whatever help we can and extend the loving hand of friendship that can help them cross over to peace and security.

And while we are on this subject, may I appeal to you, be a friend to all, be a friend of humanity in this sad world that is smitten with suffering! May the warmth of your friendship radiate towards all people who cross your path; may your good cheer and helpful attitude put a smile on their lips! May you be a helper and healer of all who suffer and are in pain!

Exercise:

What is the worst crisis you have faced in your life? Did you handle it alone? Or were you blessed enough to have supportive friends who were with you during the tough times?

What is it that you would have liked to receive from your friends in that situation, which perhaps was not available to you? What did you feel was lacking?

What was it that you appreciated most about your friends in that crisis?

Are you, as a friend, capable of offering these qualities to others?

Always be ready to offer help: A friend in need is a friend indeed!

Practical Suggestion 5

Make your advice constructive:
Don't offer advice that you
cannot follow yourself

How to Become Wise

How to Become Wise:

Once, a friend asked Mullah Nasruddin: "Nasruddin, how does one become wise?"

Nasruddin replied promptly, "Listen attentively to wise people when they speak. And when someone is listening to you, listen attentively to what you are saying!"

Advice is like snow; the softer it falls, the longer it dwells upon, and the deeper it sinks into the mind.

Samuel Taylor Coleridge

Make your advice constructive: Don't offer advice that you cannot follow yourself.

"What do you do with all the good advice you receive?" someone asked Oscar Wilde.

"I always pass it on," replied Mr. Wilde. "It's the only thing you can do with advice. It is never of any use to oneself."

With due respect to the hundreds of people who give others sound advice, with appropriate courtesy to relationship experts and counselors who have dispensed advice to people in difficulties, it must be admitted, that we remember with deep gratitude throughout our lives, not people who gave us solutions, answers and remedies, but those who reached out to us with a reassuring touch and a gesture of support!

"Wise men don't need advice," said Benjamin Franklin. "Fools won't take it."

Please do not get this wrong. I am not disparaging good advice. All of us need it at some time or the other in our lives. I only mean to say that 'empty' advice without supportive actions and gestures is not of great value to anyone.

We live in a world today where professional, expert advice is available to all of us who can afford to pay for it, whether it has to do with paying or evading tax, buying or selling shares, choosing Medicine or Engineering as a career, staying married or opting for divorce, ending or carrying on with relationships. In such a professionalised (commercialised) environment, what is the value that attaches to personal advice from people who are close to us?

Friends tell me that over and above professional experts, there is also a lot of 'online' advice available on dating, making matches and finding partners available on the internet. Surely what we have here is excess, rather than dearth! I am reminded of the wise Frenchman who remarked that the one thing people are most generous with is – advice! And there is nothing that people take more reluctantly than advice!

And yet, how many of us can say that we have passed through our life up to this point in time without ever having asked our friends, "What do you think…?"

We have dwelt on all the negative aspects of good advice. It is time to focus on the positives now. We need good counsel; we need an outside perspective on our problems and difficulties. Who better to give it to us than our friends? Whether in crucial decision-making, heart-to-heart discussions or in crisis situations, we turn to our friends with the query, "What should I do?"

Once that question is posed to us, we can be sure that we are not going to proffer unwanted, unsolicited advice. Our counsel, our suggestion is being sought in all trust and honesty. This does not give us the freedom to let loose a volley of do's and don'ts and sit in judgment on our friend's sins of omission and commission. Rather, it is up to us to consider our friend's situation with due care and diligence and weigh the best course of action that is open to him. Remember, our best advantage as the one who gives advice is this: we can look at it from a different perspective. But we are friends; not professional counselors; therefore, we must think and speak with empathy; that is, put ourselves in our friend's shoes and understand his predicament and his limitations.

That is tough, isn't it? If we take this into consideration, we will not fall into the category of those people who liberally give advice that they themselves can never follow!

Experts and counselors obviously adopt an approach that we cannot follow. In a sense, we are involved, because it is our friend we are trying to help. This calls for detachment and empathy, involvement and patience, understanding and objectivity.

Perhaps these are some steps that we may consider in such situations:

1. Put kindness and concern before words. Let your advice be offered with love rather than severity.

2. If it is an emotional problem you are dealing with, don't adopt the role of the amateur psychiatrist; don't take on yourself the task of prescribing therapies. Remember that it is your friend you are dealing with, not a case study.

3. Allow your friend to say all that he needs to express. Permit him to feel a sense of release and listen to him without interruption so that he feels lighter.

4. Be honest; if you feel that you cannot help in a particular situation, suggest gently that you may seek professional help. In serious cases such as drug addiction or alcoholism, laymen cannot be of much use.

5. Make sure that what you are offering is collaborative and cooperative; not judgmental or superior. Your approach should be "Let's try this…" rather than "You should have…"

6. Don't offer multiple hypothetical options; your friend does not need text book advice on how to break up with his wife or how to settle a legal dispute with his bank. He wants your support and practical help.

Make your advice constructive: Don't offer advice that you cannot follow yourself.

7. Your friend may be in an emotional crisis; you are not. Therefore, weigh the consequences of the advice you are offering; if your friend is vulnerable enough to follow your advice blindly, it is up to you to weigh the pros and cons and ensure that there will not be a negative backlash. Consider both short-term and long-term consequences.

8. Never ever give advice that you yourself will not follow! This is the ultimate test of sound advice.

9. Sometimes, people are looking to you for decision support. In this case, what they need more than all else is information that can help them decide. So go out and get the required information that can help your friend.

10. All personal advice is subjective. Make sure you separate facts from opinions before you recommend any course of action.

Let us admit, it is both a great honour and a great responsibility when friends turn to us for advice. Your advice must be empowering, rather than overpowering! Sound and sensible advice can help our friends make the right choices, take the right decisions and solve problems in a mature and methodical way. Ill-thought advice, rashly given, can have disastrous consequences for our friends and our friendship! So let us weigh our words carefully. Let us be honest enough to admit to ourselves and to our friends that we do not have all the right answers. There are no readymade solutions to life's problems. Every situation, every individual who confronts a situation is unique. Therefore, let compassion and understanding be the basis of your advice.

Exercise:

Look back on your life and think of all the advice that you have received from others. What did you find really useful? What was the least useful and most annoying?

Was it the platitudes that people uttered?

Was it the I-told-you-so attitude?

Was it that unrealistic "Things will sort themselves out" approach?

Do you bear these in mind when it is your turn to offer advice?

Do you offer empowering advice or overpowering advice?

Practical Suggestion 6

Be a Good Listener

What's Music Without Listeners?

A long time ago, in China there were two friends, one who played the harp skillfully and one who listened skillfully. When the one played or sang about a mountain, the other would say: "I can see the mountain before us." When the one played about water, the listener would exclaim: "Here is the running stream!"

But the listener fell sick and died. The first friend cut the strings of his harp and never played again. Since that time the cutting of harp strings has always been a sign of intimate friendship.

Zen Flesh, Zen Bones

Most people do not listen with the intent to understand; they listen with the intent to reply.

Stephen R. Covey

I request my readers to answer this question honestly: What is your favourite topic of conversation? What is it that you love to talk about most?

May I give you the answer? People love to talk about themselves. Mothers and lovers may be the exception in that they love to talk about their children/loved ones; but in reality, they are talking about their feelings for the loved ones!

We listen to music; we listen to our friends on the cellphone; students listen to lectures; we have no choice but to listen to our superiors at work. No one can accuse us of not listening. The question is: are we listening with our ears as well as with our minds and hearts?

Given the choice, most people would rather talk than listen! Little wonder then that listening is the most neglected of skills. Most of us are highly inefficient as listeners. We miss much of what is said and forget much of what we hear. Listening or rather, the lack of listening, has been identified as one of the most frequent problems in marriages, social relationships and even in job situations.

Most of us are indeed, blessed with a sound sense of hearing: but that does not mean that we are good listeners!

Listening to your friends is one of the most essential requisites of true friendship. Take the time to listen to your friend; understand his needs and you will be amazed by the appreciation your friend feels for just allowing him to open up! Sometimes, that is all they need at a particular moment, just patient, empathetic listening, rather than advice or help.

But most of the time, we do not listen with empathy; we do not even listen with the intention of understanding: we are only listening to prepare our response – our 'take' on the subject!

Active or Empathic Listening is listening to understand the speaker's needs, wants and feelings, so that you can appreciate his/her point of view.

The Tao of Communication tells us: "Knowledge speaks, but wisdom listens". And again, "Be a good listener; your ears will never get you into trouble".

I often tell my friends that the greatest famine in the world today is the famine of understanding. No two people seem to understand each other today! Therefore, misunderstandings abound in our age. There is misunderstanding in our homes, our clubs, our schools, colleges, universities, corporations and organisations.

Be a Good Listener

I recall the words of the great Parsi Prophet, Zoroaster: "Know well that a hundred temples of wood and stone have not the value of one understanding heart!"

Understanding hearts are what we need, so that people may live and work in harmonious, peaceful co-existence! And understanding our friends begins with empathetic listening.

If you wish to enrich your relationships, learn to be a good listener. Let the other person talk and prove his point to his satisfaction. Do not interrupt him while he is talking, even if he is your subordinate. Wouldn't you feel exasperated if someone interrupts what you are trying to say?

"Please let me finish!" are the words uttered most frequently at committee meetings.

Let us listen more, talk less.

We were made to listen: that is why God has given us two ears and only one mouth. If we had been given two mouths on either side of our heads and just one ear on our face, how funny we would look!

Be a good listener; therefore, listen not only with your ears, but with your heart. Menfolk, especially bosses and husbands, need to work on their listening skills.

It is a great privilege to have friends who trust you and wish to share their personal problems with you. For good friends, talking to one another is almost like thinking aloud; such is their sense of trust and confidence in each other. Your friend may use you as a 'sounding board' for new ideas and business ventures. But the role of the listener in this case cannot be passive; you have to listen, understand, sometimes counter and question, to help your friends achieve clarity in their ideas. You can also offer constructive ideas and suggestions.

There are other kinds of listening situations. We turn to our friends when we are burdened by personal problems, which, for some reason, we cannot discuss with family members. Many teenagers think their friends understand them better than their mothers or fathers. In some cases, it might be family problems that they wish to share with you or some emotional issue that is making them sad. In such cases, just listen without interrupting or offering your comments. Hear them out fully. Allow them to give full expression to whatever is troubling them – their fears, frustrations, insecurities or more tangible problems.

Look them in the eye as they speak. Do not forget to send nonverbal signals like sympathetic nods, gestures that will aid their unburdening process. At this stage, refrain from giving advice.

It is a bad idea, at such times, to respond with a story of your own, however similar it may be! Allow the focus to be on your friend; let him get your full attention. Ask gently probing questions that will allow them to elaborate on their feelings. Your listening should be cathartic for them. During such situations, please devote all your attention to them. Do not feign or pretend interest. Be genuine. By the very act of empathetic listening, you are helping your friend a great deal! By giving him the chance to talk freely and be heard with sympathy, you will help him reach greater clarity and reassurance.

It is important that we must not be dismissive about their feelings. Their fears and insecurities are real to them, and we have to offer them affection and understanding. Telling them that they are being foolish or imagining the worst will only isolate them. And even if they do tend to exaggerate their problems, you can assure them that things will get better.

Most important of all, stay connected to your friend. Many young people have no patience with others' problems these days. But this is especially callous and insensitive in friendship. Learn to listen with your ears – as well as your mind and heart. Listen with love, compassion and understanding. Advice and help and further action can come later!

Exercise:

Next time a friend starts talking to you about his problems, respond with "Tell me more."

That is a signal that you are in a listening mode; no friend can fail to appreciate this.

Ask questions to clarify your understanding: "What do you want to accomplish?" or "What is your concern?" or whatever fits the situation.

Listen carefully and suspend judgment.

Be a Good Listener

Practical Suggestion 7

Learn to appreciate your friends

The Moonlight Sonata

Ludwig Von Bethoven was one of the greatest musicians the world has known. At the age of 11 he began to compose his music, and in his teens he won fame and fortune as a great composer.

One evening, Beethoven was passing a cobbler's cottage, when he heard someone practising one of his compositions. As he paused to listen, he heard a girl exclaim, "I wish I could hear a real musician playing this piece, so that I could learn to render it properly!"

Beethoven entered the cottage and found a young girl seated at a piano. She was blind. Offering to play for her, he sat at the piano and played for an hour or so.

The girl was enthralled! Her appreciation fired the enthusiasm of Beethoven, and he went on playing. Dusk had set in; the cottage grew dark but the silvery moonlight filtered into the room. Under its inspiration and the whole-hearted warmth of the girl's appreciation, Beethoven composed his famous Moonlight Sonata.

Feeling gratitude and not expressing it is like wrapping a present and not giving it.

William Arthur Ward

Learn to Appreciate Your Friends

It was William James who said that the deepest need of a human being is the craving to be appreciated.

Human relationships thrive on caring, sharing and mutual appreciation. We rely on our loved ones, our friends and those closest to us, for moral support and encouragement. The amazing thing is that appreciation costs us nothing. It requires hardly any effort. A smile, a warm gesture, a word of praise is all it takes; and yet we are so reluctant to offer it to others…

No one knows who originally wrote or said these lines, but all of us have read these lines and have been inspired by them. I'm sure you have heard them too.

I shall pass through this world but once. Any good, therefore, that I can do, or any kindness that I can show to any human being, let me do it now. Let me not defer nor neglect it, for I shall not pass this way again.

Any kindness that I can show to any human being… The popular writer Dale Carnegie calls this one of the basic requirements for happiness in life. "Cut out this quotation and put it where you will see it every morning!" he tells us.

Is it not true that all of us feel happy when we are appreciated? In this, as in other things, what we send out comes back to us. For life is like a boomerang: what we are, what we do, comes back to us. When we give our best to the world, when we send out warmth, love and appreciation – it all comes back to us.

The great artist of the Renaissance, Leonardo da Vinci said: "Never reprove a friend in public. Always praise him in front of others." When you appreciate others, you help to draw out the best in them. This leads to happiness all around.

Above all, appreciate people! Human relationships need to be nurtured. We often think of our friends, spouses and parents as 'pillars of strength' which are always there for our solid support. I urge you, occasionally think of them as precious plants that need constant tending! When tensions are rising and troubles are mounting, it is people who are close to us that bear the brunt of our stress. We are often courteous, polite and kind to perfect strangers, but rude and brusque to our own spouses and parents. And it is often our friends who receive the brunt of our bad moods.

It is not enough to feel appreciation. Express your appreciation in words and deeds. This will make your life fresh and interesting!

The neighbour who greets you a with bright smile and cheerful hello...

A Thank you card from a friend who was pleased and touched by your gift…

A box of chocolates which your colleague offers you...

A friend who asks you with genuine care and concern, "How are you?"...

And, not to forget my young friends, let me add:

An e-card with music from a friend who knows that you are feeling low...

Lovely smileys and lots of laughing emotions in a text message from a friend who has been away...

A really good joke or a funny cartoon on MMS from friends who love to make you laugh...

Every day we are witness to acts of loving kindness offered to us. Let us not dismiss them as small or trivial. They deserve to be appreciated!

Every now and then, all of us need to hear someone say to us, "I think you are wonderful!" And we need to say this to our friends, our colleagues and co-workers, our parents, spouses and children.

Why don't you utter these magic words of appreciation to someone today?

Dale Carnegie tells us, "Three-fourths of all the people you will ever meet are hungering and thirsting for appreciation. Give it to them and they will love you!" Indeed, appreciative words are the greatest incentive for doing good work.

When you tell your child, husband or friend that they are wrong, that they are insensitive or that they have done something badly, you take away their incentive for improvement. On the other hand, when you are liberal with your encouragement and appreciation, they will do their best and surprise you with what they can achieve!

Making others feel good about themselves builds better relationships. This is what Lord Chesterfield urges his son to do: Make every person like himself a little better and he or she will begin to like you very much. Sincere praise reassures people. It dissolves the negative notions they have about themselves and improves their self-esteem.

It is our besetting fault that we often take others for granted. We eat what is placed on the table but fail to appreciate the person who cooked the meal. We lean on our friends for support, cry on their shoulders but fail to appreciate them for always being there for us.

Silent gratitude is not of much use to anyone. Therefore learn to express your appreciation. It is not enough to think that someone is being kind and good; a kind word unsaid is a kind thought wasted. Go up to people; reach out to praise them,

Learn to Appreciate Your Friends

thank them, appreciate them for what they have done and you will really make a difference!

The popular comedian Jimmy Durant was entertaining a packed auditorium of wounded soldiers in a Stanton Island War Hospital. The soldiers were so appreciative that there were several 'encores' at the end of the programme.

During those thunderous ovations and applause, Durant's secretary kept on making anxious signals to the actor. They had to leave for New York as soon as possible – for he had two very important programmes scheduled there the next day.

Durant noticed his desperate signals and mouthed a silent NO. He pointed to his secretary two wounded soldiers in the front now, who were laughing heartily and enjoying the show thoroughly. Each one of them had an arm amputated – and they were clapping with their remaining hands, one on the other.

"I have never received such an appreciation in my life!" Durant whispered.

He went on to entertain the wounded soldiers throughout the night.

Appreciate your friends! They are rare and invaluable, because they have allowed you to be yourself. They do not love you for your utility value; they love you for what you are. When you feel gratitude, your blessings multiply. When you show gratitude, your friends multiply.

Exercise:

What is it that you appreciate most about your friends?

Their love and loyalty? Their confidence and trust? Their mere presence when you need them?

Do your friends have special qualities like patience, a sense of humour or a systematic approach?

Have you told them that you appreciate these qualities?

Digital appreciation for the smartphone age

Practical Suggestion 8

Discuss issues: but do not argue!

Inside or Outside?

Fa-yen, a Chinese Zen teacher, overheard four monks arguing heatedly about subjectivity and objectivity. He joined them and said: "There is a big stone lying here on the ground. Do you consider it to be inside or outside your mind"?

One of the monks replied: "From the Buddhist viewpoint everything is an objectification of mind, so I would say that the stone is inside my mind."

"Your head must feel very heavy," observed Fa-yen, "if you are carrying around a stone like that in your mind."

'Seek first to be understanding,

then to be understood'.

Most people don't listen. Not really. They listen long enough to devise a solution to the speaker's problem or a rejoinder to what's being said. Then they dive into the conversation. You'll be more effective in your relationships with people if you sincerely try to understand them fully before you try to make them understand your point of view.

Stephen Covey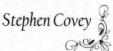

When Jesus's disciples got into an argument over who was holy and who would get places in heaven, Jesus said to them: 'Whosoever desires to become great among you shall be your servant. And whosoever of you desires to be first, shall be the slave of all. For even the Son of Man did not come to be served, but to serve, and to sacrifice His life as a ransom for many'.

Let us ask ourselves: How many of us will be prepared to accept such a role? How many of us will do our best, in our allotted sphere of life, without worrying about winning, influencing and riding roughshod over others? Can we live and work and do whatever we can to promote peace and harmony rather than push our own points of view across? Can we hold our opinions and convictions without trying to push them down others' throats? Then we will, indeed, be truly blessed!

In the English Language writing exercises we are often asked to write both 'discussion' essays and 'argumentative' essays. In the former, we look at both sides of the proposition; in the latter, we support one view. This is a legitimate training in presenting perspectives, balancing opinions and marshaling support in favour of a particular position.

Alas, in real life, people are not so balanced in arguments! For many of us, it is easy to take up just one side of an argument and express a strong opinion on it. Discussion invariably remains rational, cool and logical. But an argument can become emotionally driven. Sad to say, the participants sometimes end up shouting at (shouting down) each other!

Arguments generally lead nowhere. One person or the other may think he has won; but actually he has only shouted down or silenced the other person, not into acceptance or submission, but into antagonism and hostility. Civility and courtesy are the first casualties in a heated argument. Friendships (and other relationships) are the next to fall.

Friends do not always agree on everything. It is perfectly possible for them to disagree on issues and still continue to respect each other's opinion. In fact disagreement is common in all relationships. Members of a family cannot agree on which T.V channels to watch; friends disagree on politics; even colleagues disagree on business strategy. Experts say that this creates an open environment and prevents what is known as "tunnel vision".

Discuss issues: But do not Argue!

Laugh it off!

How to handle arguments?

Grandpa was celebrating his 100th birthday and everybody complimented him on how athletic and well- preserved he appeared.

"I will tell you the secret of my success," he cackled. "My wife and I were married 75 years ago. On our wedding night, we made a solemn pledge. Whenever we had an argument, the one who lost would go outside and take a walk. Gentlemen, I have been in the open air day after day for some 75 years now."

Lou Goldstein tells us: "A disagreement is a chance for knowledge… while an argument is an exchange of ignorance." For good measure, he adds, "Either you control your attitude, or allow it to control you and end up losing a friend".

We waste our energy in unnecessary discussions and debates. In such discussions there is always a person with an egoistic bent of mind, whose sole purpose is in challenging and debating to win his argument. Such futile activities take us away from the track of true friendship.

For the purpose of our discussion on friendship, let me reiterate this: sometimes, a disagreement turns into an argument and ends up as a fight. It is up to us to ensure that as friends, we can continue to hold civilised discussions that don't degenerate into catfights and quarrels. I cannot help thinking that it would be a very boring world indeed, if all of us agreed on everything and thought alike on all subjects! It would only lead to intellectual stagnation.

While it is healthy to disagree, I would nevertheless caution you on the following:

1. Do not let politics or religion become the subject of your discussions. This invariably leads to heated arguments.

2. If one of you is involved in anything that is unethical or illegal, it is time for the other to speak up.

3. Do not retaliate hastily. Of the unspoken word, you are the master; of the spoken word, you are the slave.

4. Avoid sweeping statements like "You never…" or "You always…"

Interestingly, The National Communication Association says that "the process of conflict and arguing allows us to see things from other people's points of view". In other words, it strengthens relationships, allows us to know our friends better, and helps us grow as individuals. This works fine as long as we are able to come to an amicable settlement if not a common understanding at the end of our discussions. The goal of a debate cannot be to change your friend's opinion.

Conversation and discussion are often the way friends spend their time. It can be intellectually stimulating and very enjoyable, when they are willing to listen to each other's point of view. Even when consensus is not reached, people agree to disagree. Where there is mutual respect, different perspectives are appreciated ; friends who hold divergent opinions actually broaden each another's intellectual horizons. A Group Discussion or GD as it is called among students is an intellectual exercise in logical thinking and oral communication.

When the discussion turns into an argument, in a way, the interlocutors lose control over themselves and the debate. Voices are raised; tempers flare; people begin to shout; the other person is not given a hearing; opponents are shouted down. People cannot agree to disagree in civility. Instead, they only want to make everyone else agree with them. Nothing is gained; but friends may be lost!

'Experts' have identified the following arguments which nobody can win. (I offer the list to you so that you don't get into an argument with your friend on any of these issues!)

1. Which came first, chicken or egg?
2. Does God exist?
3. Free Will or Destiny?
4. Was man created or did he evolve from lower species?
5. Should we abolish the death penalty?

Let me also sound a note of caution. Healthy discussions cause no rift. But frequent arguments are not healthy! If you find that you and your friends are constantly picking verbal fights, it is time to pause and reflect on what is happening to your friendship.

Arguments may not necessarily mean that your friendship is breaking up; but it may mean that you are changing. When friends begin to lead their own lives, when one of them gets married or moves to a different location, they begin to see things differently. Many friendships go through a transition phase at such points, but emerge stronger in course of time.

There is so much wisdom to be learned from the people around us! Life offers so many opportunities for us to evolve emotionally and intellectually. Some of us are blessed with material wealth and riches; some of us are blessed with business acumen; some are gifted with artistic bent and creativity; yet others stand apart with their caring and compassionate attitude; a few of us are efficient and capable administrators; sincerity and devotion mark the efforts of some people; the world needs us all.

We can each contribute our own special and unique efforts to make life more meaningful and beautiful. What matters is that we recognise the others' contributions and appreciate it.

All of us, with our individual gifts and skills are like so many strings on God's lute. We will make divine music, when we function together.

Exercise:

You can try the following techniques for civilised discussion:

1. Do not raise your voice unnecessarily.

2. Remain calm at all times.

3. Do not bluntly point out that your friend is wrong.

4. Always be mild and gentle in tone and attitude; show your goodwill towards your friend.

5. Never resort to verbal abuse or name calling.

Practical Suggestion 9

Make promises sparingly:
But keep them faithfully

Lifelong Friends

Xu Shaoyu lived in Qiantang Province in China. In early August, one year, he borrowed one hundred silver coins from his friend Yi Zhai. Yi would not take a receipt from his friend. Instead, Xu promised him orally, that the money would be returned one year later.

In August of the next year, Xu Shaoyu became critically ill. In a delirium, he had been talking to himself while lying in bed, "It is almost time for me to return the money. What should I do if I die?"

His wife said, "You are so ill and we have spent so much on medicine. In addition, you don't have a written document about the borrowed money. Therefore, you don't have to worry about returning the money". Xu was horrified. "He did not write a receipt because he trusted me. How can I not keep my promise?"

At last, Xu Shaoyu asked his wife to sell a piece of jade and two fur coats from their home. They got ninety silver coins. They then borrowed ten coins from others. Therefore, they returned the money on the due date. Several days later, Xu Shaoyu was completely cured. He and Yi remained lifelong friends.

Story from ancient China

Promises are like babies
easy to make, hard to deliver.

Author Unknown

Life runs smoothly all round, for all people, when people adhere to the principle of truthfulness. In the past Truth was perceived as the very foundation of a Nation. In personal life too, no one likes a man who utters lies or breaks his promises. When the sacred bond of trust is broken, relationships cannot flourish.

"...Words are very rascals since bonds disgraced them," says a character in one of Shakespeare's plays. He is referring to those times when a man's word was more binding than any legal document to which he affixed his signature. Alas, nowadays, we have little value even for bonds and promissory notes!

We have got into a state when we assert blithely, "Promises are meant to be broken"!

Promises are sacred words that attest our faith and loyalty, especially when we make them to our friends. So it is not just promises we are breaking when we fail to live up to those words; we are actually breaking the sacred bonds of trust and loyalty and truthfulness. If you feel that promises can't be kept, there is a simple solution: don't make them in the first place!

If you ask me, I would assert emphatically, promises are not meant to be broken! In fact, our words, when we 'give' them in trust to friends, are not meant to be dismissed as mere words! It is we who have invested them with the power of truth and honesty: to take away the power so invested is to declare ourselves liars and cheats! Many people all around us may be breaking promises every moment, but that does not mean that promises are meant to be broken!

'A promise made is a debt unpaid', so goes the saying. You create trust and comfort in the person to whom you make a promise. When it is broken, it is as bad as refusing the money you owe to him.

Have you ever read the words written on currency notes that we spend like water nowadays? They read: "I promise to pay the bearer the sum of ..." The currency note is an assurance from the Reserve Bank, from the Government of the country that the person who possesses the currency note can obtain paid goods worth the denomination of the note that he hands over to the seller. The currency note is just a piece of paper; it is the government's promise inscribed on the note that lends value to it, and makes it the legal tender of exchange. (On the U.S. dollar, you will find the words, "This note is a legal tender for all debts...").”

In the good old days, people actually used silver and gold coins which represented the actual worth of the amount being exchanged. The coin itself represented its

Make Promises Sparingly: But Keep them Faithfully

worth in money terms, and so no promises were made. Today's paper notes have no intrinsic value. It is just a piece of paper. That is why investors and financial wizards advice us not to hoard paper currency, but to convert it into gold or real estate or stocks and shares!

I am reminded of the words of John Burroughs, "For anything worth having one must pay the price; and the price is always work, patience, love, self-sacrifice, no paper currency, no promises to pay, but the gold of real service."

It is indeed disturbing to sound a cynical note here: counterfeit currency notes are becoming increasingly common these days... And the cynical writer Samuel Butler observes, "Oaths are but words, and words are but wind."

What is it that makes us believe oaths? When we attempt to answer that question, we will realise that it is not promises that make us trust people, it is the people who make them that make us respect and trust promises. Therefore, making promises is like holding your trust like water in your hands; the moment you slacken your fingers, the water flows away; the moment you fail your promise, your trust and sense of truth and honesty are undermined.

How many of us are aware of the sacred, inviolable bonds of truth and trust and honesty and personal integrity when we blithely make promises by the dozen?

"Eggs and oaths are easily broken" says a Danish proverb. It is we who have made current the cynical saying: promises are made only to be broken.

Do you make small and big promises to your friends, never intending to keep them (or just not serious about adhering to your words?) These promises might range from the utterly simple, "I'll be there at 6 o' clock" to "I will get the application form for you from the University," to the more serious, "Count on me, I will deliver your letter to the Manager" and the far more serious, "Trust me, your secret is safe with me."

Losers, dishonest people, untrustworthy friends make promises only to break them; winners, honest men and women, friends who are loyal and truthful always keep their promises. Winners, in this case, make good human beings and great friends; losers make excuses and utter platitudes.

What are you, a winner or a loser?

Hypocrites have no compunctions; they can make the wildest and most impossible promises, because they don't intend to keep them! Beware of friends who make repeated promises to you: he is likely to fail you. Thus, a man with a sense of humour remarked with a sigh about a youth whom he trusted: "I thought he was a young man of promise; it turns out that he is a young man of promises"!

Friendship is a sacred bond; an unspoken, unwritten contract of trust and love. If you make promises to your friends, you must keep them; and the lesser you promise and the more you deliver without promises, the stronger the friendship. There are friends who do not waste words; but their sovereign actions more than make up for verbal comfort. It is good to promise what you can perform; but it is better to deliver more than your promise. We would do well to remember Mahatma Gandhi's words: "A breach of promise is a base surrender of truth".

So what do we do when friends look to us for reassurance? Here are a few guidelines:

1. You don't always have to be a yes-person. Be honest about your capabilities and performance. "I will do my best," is better than "I will get it done."

2. Make your friend understand that there is uncertainty in life; one can only hope, not expect outcomes.

3. If you are in a situation that demands commitment, think deeply; reflect carefully before you give your word.

4. Do not over extend yourself; do not make promises knowing fully well that you cannot keep them.

Exercise:

Start making promises to yourself. It might be something as simple as, "I'll call up my parents today" or "I'll go out for a walk this evening".

Judge for yourself how far you are able to keep your own promises to yourself. Analyse the reasons why you break them.

If you break the promises repeatedly, tell yourself, "I will not make a promise that I don't intend to keep."

Cultivate inner trust. It will automatically extend outward to the people in your life.

Trust is a valuable quality. Be careful when you place it on someone else; be aware of the responsibility when someone places it on you.

It is the calling card of your character!

Make Promises Sparingly: But Keep them Faithfully

Practical Suggestion 10

Learn to accept criticism
in the right spirit

A True Friend

It is said that once, the great Caliph, Haroun-al-Rashid, arranged for a grand banquet in his palace. The banquet hall was decorated with the most expensive silk hangings and silver and gold ornaments studded with precious gems. The walls and ceiling glittered in opulence and magnificence. The dining table was laden with the most expensive silverware, and decorated with the rarest and most beautiful plants and flowers.

As for the guests, they were the who's who of Arabian nobility as well as poets, scholars, wise philosophers and musicians. A sumptuous fare was served to them, and as the guests were enjoying the feast and the distinguished company at the table, the Caliph called upon the poetic genius of his court, Abul Atayah, and said to him, "O prince among poets, give our guests a taste of your genius. Describe in your inimitable style, the grandeur of my court and the glory of this banquet."

The poet rose to the royal commandment and began with a flourish: "Long may you live, O Caliph, and enjoy thy life in the magnificent shelter of this lofty palace."

The courtiers and other guests cheered loudly and clapped their hands in appreciation.

"That is indeed a good beginning," said Rashid. "Do go on and let us hear the rest."

The poet went on: "May each new dawn herald a new happiness for you. May you see all your desires and dreams fulfilled each evening."

"Good! Wonderful!" exclaimed the Caliph, "Go on."

"May your every command be obeyed. May your mighty will reign supreme in this land."

The Caliph nodded in appreciation. "Proceed," he urged the poet.

The poet bowed his head and said: "But my Caliph, you are wise. When the hour of death comes, you will learn that all these delights were but a passing shadow."

Learn to Accept Criticism in the Right Spirit

The Caliph's eyes were filled with tears. He was overcome by intense emotion. He turned his face away and wept.

One of the King's officers rose in anger. "Enough of this!" he cried. "Stop your recitation at once. Our Master wanted to be amused with a few pleasant thoughts. But you have filled his heart with despair."

"Do not ask him to stop," said Haroun-al-Rashid. "He is a true friend. He has seen me in my blindness, and is trying to open my eyes."

> *"Criticism may not be agreeable, but it is necessary. It fulfills the same function as pain in the human body. It calls attention to an unhealthy state of things."*
>
> *Winston Churchill*

W e have spoken a great deal about truth, honesty and loyalty in friendship. When we speak of truth, it includes being able to take the truth about yourself from your friends. Your friends are less than honest if they don't tell you your shortcomings and failings as an individual. (You owe them the truth too!) But it is one thing to tell the truth; quite another thing to accept it with grace.

Even apart from truth-telling, there are occasions when our words or actions may upset our friends. This may lead to criticism of our behaviour.

How do you respond to criticism from your friends? For many of us, the first reaction is anger and denial.

Consider the following hypothetical comments:

"You should not have laughed so loudly".

"You were absolutely rude with him".

"Whatever made you raise your voice so loudly"?

Our first impulse is to deny or hit back. "Certainly not!" Or "You are exaggerating."

We are all slaves of our ego. Criticism hits where it hurts most. It wounds our sense of vanity and pride and dents our image of being right and fair and just at all times. We are demoralised when we realise that others perceive us to be different.

But as we realise in our logical minds, criticism can be taken very positively. Instead of letting criticism control us we can take a command over criticism by taking it in the right spirit, as a helpful and constructive feedback, and setting out to conquer our own weaknesses and failings.

It was a wise man who reminded us: "It is well to remember that the entire population of the universe, with one trifling exception, is composed of others". People who are genuinely humble, know that the 'others' are significant; they know that many of these 'others' can be pretty intelligent and interesting. They know that there is a lot they can learn from other people; therefore, they treat everyone with respect and courtesy. They are keen and eager to discover what other people can offer. They are fascinated by how others think, how others feel differently from them, and what different approaches they adopt to solving problems. And when they get feedback from others that is not positive, they mend their weaknesses.

Learn to Accept Criticism in the Right Spirit

Gautama the Buddha tells us: "They who speak much are blamed. They who speak a little are blamed. They who are silent are also blamed. In this world there is none who is not blamed."

The Buddha himself was indifferent to both praise and blame. Perhaps no other spiritual leader was so reviled, so abused as he. But he never, ever retaliated.

On one occasion the Buddha was invited by a rich merchant for alms to his house. But when he arrived there, instead of entertaining Him, the merchant began to heap the vilest abuse on him.

The Buddha politely inquired, "Do you often entertain visitors to your house, dear man?"

"Frequently," the man replied.

"What do you do when they come?"

"Oh, we prepare a sumptuous feast."

"If they fail to turn up, what then?"

"Why, what a foolish question! We eat it all up!"

"Well, good man, you have invited me for alms and entertained me with abuse. I accept nothing. Please take it back."

Once, the Buddha was accused of murdering a woman assisted by His disciples. His detractors severely criticised the Buddha and His Disciples to such an extent that the Venerable Ananda suggested to the Buddha that they should leave for another village.

" But what, Ananda, if those villagers also abuse us?"

"Well then, Lord, we will proceed to another village."

"Then Ananda, the whole of India will have no place for us. Be patient. These abuses will automatically cease."

These are memorable lessons for all.

Venerable Narada Mahathera, The Buddha and His Teachings

We gain from others when we realise that as human beings, we are all inter-dependent. We learn from others when we realise that we need their help, and seek the same with humility. And help can also come in the form of constructive criticism! At such times, we come to realise how little we know, and how we cannot get on without others. However, we would miss these valuable insights, if our pride and ego stand in our way.

There is so much wisdom to be learned from the people around us! Life offers so many opportunities for us to evolve emotionally and intellectually. Some of us are blessed with material wealth and riches; some of us are blessed with business acumen; some are gifted with artistic bent and creativity; yet others stand apart with their caring and compassionate attitude; a few of us are efficient and capable administrators; sincerity and devotion mark the efforts of some people; the world needs us all.

We can each contribute our own special and unique efforts to make life more meaningful and beautiful. What matters is that we recognise the others' contributions and appreciate it; that we accept their views and benefit from it. Therefore the saying goes: "Two heads are better than one".

How can you take criticism from your friends in the right spirit? So here are a few suggestions:

1. Listen to the feedback with patience and humility. Realise that it is for your own benefit.

2. Do not react on a hasty impulse. Allow the remarks, however negative they may be, to sink in.

3. Find the positives in criticism. Look at it as an opportunity to learn something new and improve yourself in the bargain.

4. Appreciate the honesty of your friends in voicing their criticism and actually thank them for telling you a few home truths. This makes all the difference to your relationship.

5. Draw the maximum benefit from your friend's honesty – actually go out and try to improve yourself!

6. Don't take criticism personally. Detach the criticism from yourself and only look at the actions or behavior that has been criticized.

Even the most evolved and intellectual people are upset by criticism when they first hear it. Sensitive people shut it out altogether and retreat into a shell. We are all vulnerable in this aspect and being hurt at first is understandable. But we will do well to remember that accepting all feedback in the right spirit will only make us more successful and more easy to get on with!

Exercise:

Here is a four-step guide to taking criticism gracefully:

1. Respect your friend's opinion. Give him a patient hearing.
2. Internalise the feedback. Reflect on it and evaluate its merits.
3. Follow up with positive action. Set out to improve.
4. Take the initiative! Don't wait for criticism. Ask your friends to evaluate your performance/actions and give you a feedback.

Make God Your Best Friend!

"It was only a Woodcutter!"

There was a man who met me. He said to me, "I do not believe in God. I do not believe in prayers. I have never ever prayed to God, even once in all my life."

I asked him, "Are you sure you have never prayed to God even once in all your life?"

He thought for a few moments and said, "Yes, I remember, I offered a prayer once."

"And when was that?" I asked him.

"When I was a little boy," he said, "I had lost my way in the forest. I ran here and there, I shouted for help. I was terrified! Scared and shivering, in that desperate mood, I cried out, 'Oh God, if You really exist, show me the way out of this place. Let me reach home safely.'"

"What happened then?" I urged him.

"Nothing," he said.

"That's not possible," I said gently. "How could nothing have happened? Surely something must have happened, or you wouldn't be here before me. You must have found your way back to the house on that fateful day. God must have heard your prayer, surely."

"No," denied the man vehemently. "Well, yes, I did get home safely, but it had nothing to do with God! He did not come to my help. I was so scared, I sat down under a tree and just cried. God did not hear me, I tell you! But a woodcutter came along. He happened to be passing by, and he told me, he felt an urge to pass through that part of the forest. So there he was. He took my hand and led me out of the forest. It was only a woodcutter, who saved me. Not God!"

"Only a woodcutter!" I exclaimed. "What do you expect God to look like? Did you expect a man in white flowing garments with a long beard? Did you not realise that He heard your prayer and came to your rescue in the form of a woodcutter?

The Lord is my shepherd, I shall not want.

He maketh me to lie down in green pastures: He leadeth me beside the still waters.

He restoreth my soul: He leadeth me in the paths of righteousnes, for His name's sake.

Yea, though I walk through the valley of the shadow of death, I will fear no evil: for Thou art with me, Thy rod and Thy staff, they comfort me.

Thou preparest a table before me, in the presence of mine enemies: Thou anointest my head with oil, my cup runneth over.

Surely goodness and mercy shall follow me all the days of my life: and I will dwell in the house of the Lord forever.

Psalm 23, King James Bible

Make God Your Best Friend!

The best beloved poet-saint of Sind, Shah Abdul Latif, has the following words in one of his moving songs:

Thou art the Friend, the Healer Thou,

For every suffering, the remedy...

Is this not true, that in every suffering, it is God who abides with us?

Therefore, let us call out to Him in times of distress: He is the friend who will never ever let us down!

Twameva Mata Cha Pitha Twameva,

Twameva Bandhu Cha Sakha Twameva,

Twameva Vidya Dravinam Twameva

Twameva Sarvam Mama Deva Deva

Thou art my father and mother, Thou my relative and friend, Thou art my wisdom and wealth, Thou art my all!

The saints spoke nothing but the truth. They conveyed the most profound lessons of life in an utterly simple and direct language. God is our friend. He is the helper of the helpless. Trust Him!

God, the Friend of friends. He is a Friend to us all. Call Him. Seek His help. He will never fail you!

Whenever we are in trouble, whenever we are hard pressed, when we are surrounded by adverse circumstances, when we are passing through a dark night when not a single star doth shine, when we suffer from a disease that the doctors declare as incurable, when we face a financial crisis and are on the verge of bankruptcy, when we are involved in problems of personal relationships, what do we do? We call upon friends; we run to our relatives; we turn to our lawyers, doctors, to government and police officer, but we don't go to God.

But there comes a time in every one's life, when one needs His support above all others. When others fail, God who never fails us, becomes the only Source of support. Knock on His door. He will surely help you in your darkest hour of crisis.

One of the reasons why we do not turn to Him spontaneously is because God has not become real to us. To many of us, God is a distant being. He is a far off, shadowy presence, dwelling on a distant star. I ask so many people, "Where dwelleth God?"

With an uplifted finger, they point to the heavens above, as though God dwelt way beyond our reach. True, God dwells in the heavens above, but there is not a nook, not a corner on the earth, where He does not dwell.

I recall the words which are attributed to Jesus. These are not found in the Gospels, but in a less well-known eastern account of Jesus. We are told that Jesus said: "God does not dwell in the heavens above; for if so, birds will reach Him sooner than man. God does not dwell in the depths of the ocean, if so, the fishes would be able to reach Him sooner than man. God is within you. The Kingdom of God is within you."

It was Tennyson who said: "Closer is He to us than breathing, nearer than hands and feet." What a tremendous blessing this is, that God is so close to us, and that He is always available to us! We can go to Him at any time of the day or night, without previously having to fix an appointment with Him. And we can share with Him the deepest, innermost secrets of our hearts, without any hesitation or reservation. Others may laugh at us, belittle our fears and worries, call us childish or foolish. But we can be sure that God will understand us. For He loves us much more than we can ever imagine. His love is understanding; it is patient; it is forgiving. We can go to Him anytime we like, but we go everywhere else except to Him!

You must believe firstly, that God is all around you. You do not have to go to a particular place to meet Him. It is always good to go to temples, mosques and churches. But it is not only in these shrines that you can contact God. He is right in front of you, wherever you may be. All you have to do is to close your eyes, shut out the world, open your heart and call Him with deep love and longing, and there He is with you!

We need to know God. We need to move close to Him. We need to make God real in our daily lives!

But let me say to you, don't wait till you are desperate and drowning neck deep in crisis! Knock at His door when you are happy, prosperous and contented. Forge your link of love with Him when times are good. Build your relationship with God while the sun shines on you. You don't need a special appointment to meet Him! Begin with a thought of love, a thought of gratitude for all the good things in your life. Begin with His Name on your lips: start with a simple incantation or a prayer or a holy verse from the scriptures: or recite a *mantra* which brings you peace: or a verse of the famous hymn, "Thou who failest not, abide with me"! You can choose a line from inspirational poetry as that of Shah Abdul Latif, "In my darkest hour, Lord! You are my support, my stay, my all!" Or a line from the Sikh Scripture: "How can one who is under Your protection be struck with sorrow?"

Make God Your Best Friend!

"If God had taken the form, for example, of a rare, enormously large green bird, with a red beak, that perched in a tree on the embankment and perhaps even whistled in an unprecedented manner – then [the modern man] surely would have had his eyes opened," says Kierkegaard, the rationalist philosopher.

Let me say to you: how many times has your mother or father, spouse or beloved, girl friend or boy friend, son or daughter uttered to you the words, "I love you!"
What is your response when you hear the words?

Do you say, "Give it to me in writing"? Do you insist that they prove it? Proving may take eternity; believing requires just a moment, a leap of faith. Take that leap of faith. Make God your best friend!

A special word for my young friends: you really don't have to go out in search of God! God is in you, God is in your friends, God is in everyone you meet. This awareness is enough to get you close to God. Extend your hand of friendship to all, and you will find that God grasps it firmly!

Sri Ramakrishna once remarked, 'I wondered why should be God meditated upon only with eyes closed, He should be seen all around us in all human beings even with eyes wide open!'

Please do not think of God as a supplier and personal financier! As Swami Vivekananda tells us, God knows what we need, and He is sure to give it to us. We can't expect Him to take care of our greed!

When I Asked God for Strength
He Gave Me Difficult Situations to Face

When I Asked God for Brain & Brown
He Gave Me Puzzles in Life to Solve

When I Asked God for Happiness
He Showed Me Some Unhappy People

When I Asked God for Wealth
He Showed Me How to Work Hard

When I Asked God for Favors
He Showed Me Opportunities to Work Hard

When I Asked God for Peace
He Showed Me How to Help Others

God Gave Me Nothing I Wanted
He Gave Me Everything I Needed."

Swami Vivekananda

Establish your direct hotline to God. Put him on the speed dial mode in the smart device that is your heart. Talk to him in your prayers, instead of reciting set verses!

God does not care for the form, the shape, the vocabulary of our prayer. It is the feeling, the emotion that counts.

You don't have to be learned or highly educated to be able to pray. Indeed, too much learning or education, far from being a help, becomes a hindrance in the way of prayer. Sri Ramakrishna was illiterate; he could not sign his name. Yet he prayed, for hours together. He prayed as one who stood in the presence of God, speaking to Him as a child would speak to its mother.

"Have you seen God?" he was asked.

"Yes," he answered. "More clearly than I see you!"

Truly has it been said, that God who made the world has no trouble being seen and heard by those who honestly want to know Him.

What is prayer? Prayer is waiting upon God in love and longing. Without this, repetition of set prayers will not take us far. So often, prayers are read from books; they are good in as much as they draw our attention to God. But this is only the first step.

Once you have built the link through recitation or incantation of a holy *mantra,* it is easy to approach God for help. It is like going across to your best friend and unburdening yourself. Once the problem is shared, nature will provide the solution. It is as simple as 'Ask and you shall be given'. The solution to your problems already exists in the universe. It will manifest itself when you seek God's help.

God is omnipresent and omnipotent! He weaves through every breeze: He wakes in every leaf: He smiles in every flower. He has no contact address, for He is

Make God Your Best Friend!

everywhere and in everything! For the lay man, such conceptualisation is difficult. Hence, God who is formless, assumes many forms and His energy becomes manifest in different deities, gods and goddesses, whom you can make your *ishtadevata!*

You would indeed, be fortunate and truly blessed if you could find a true Guru: for that is the best way to link with God, through a realised soul, who has already formed a lasting link with Him! May God lead you to such an evolved soul!

Prayer of St. Anselm of Canterbury
Teach me to seek you,
and reveal yourself to me as I seek;
for unless you instruct me
I cannot seek you,
and unless you reveal yourself
I cannot find you.
Let me seek you in desiring you;
let me desire you in seeking you.
Let me find you in loving you;
let me love you in finding you.

God is our true friend, our guardian and our guide. Let us always seek His help, before turning to worldly sources for support.

Over the years, there is one way I have discovered to connect with the Divine, and I believe it has really drawn me closer to the Lord. I would like to share it with you. It is to sit in silence, in the calm and quiet stillness of the night, before you retire to bed, and go over all the events of the last twelve hours. Start anti-clockwise: at 10 pm or 9 pm (which is just past) and recall your actions during the day that is just over.

Ask yourself: What have I done during the day that is just over?

For some of you, the day might involve questions such as the following:

What was the action I did before I retired to my bed? Was I just watching TV? Or was I spending precious free time with the members of my family?

How and where did I eat my meal, seated with the family around the dinner table, or taking my plate to sit in front of the TV?

How did I spend my evening? Slouched over a newspaper, or reading a good book?

Seated like a zombie before the computer screen, or chatting with my siblings?

How useful was my day? How many people did I reach out to?

In what frame of mind did I leave work? Irritable and exhausted, or with the sense of having accomplished a day's useful activity?

How did I behave with my colleagues at work? Was I annoyed and suspicious about them, or did I appreciate what they did?

How did I treat my subordinates? Was I kind and courteous at all times, or did I use harsh words to criticise them?

In what frame of mind did I enter the office this morning, with the feeling that work is worship, or feeling lousy about my job and my colleagues?

The routine I have given above, is only an indication. You must fill in details of your own daily schedule. Was I kind and loving to the children? Did I attend all my lectures and pay attention to what was being taught? Was I helpful and polite to my customers? How often did I lose my temper? How often did I speak/think harshly? How many people did I refuse to meet?

Think in the reverse direction. You will realise the mistakes you have made, knowingly or unknowingly. Call God, seek His guidance. Ask Him to forgive you; ask Him to help you to forgive yourself. Ask Him to help you become a better person tomorrow; ask Him for the gift of a more worthwhile life tomorrow.

Pray to God, 'O Lord! Forgive me my faults; forgive my mistakes which I have committed in the last 24 hours. Give me the strength to correct them. Dear God, bestow on me the awareness of the true purpose of my life, and the wisdom to improve my *karma* and to do good deeds!'

In today's world of speed and stress, life has become very uncertain. It would be no exaggeration to say that people who leave home in the morning do not always return to their family in the evening. Fatal accidents are increasing, day by day. Fortunes are made and lost on the stock exchange. Cyber frauds are looting people's bank accounts from thousands of miles away. Irate mobs attack and fatally wound innocent citizens and hapless passers-by in troubled areas. Reputed companies declare insolvency and hundreds of workers lose their livelihood overnight.

Strange, unknown viruses attack children and old people, and doctors are unable to locate the right remedies to treat them.

Connecting with God can protect you and your family from untold, unheard of troubles like those I have listed above. Should such mishaps occur in your life, God's infinite mercy can guard you from the worst consequences. Therefore, I say to you: make God your best friend; seek Him; seek His protection; seek His never-failing support and help!

How may we know God? How may we draw closer to God?

All we need to do is let go of the lower self, the ego with its passion and pride, and let God in. For He is our true Self, and we are a part of His divine aspect.

When the mind is stilled, we find God in everything; and we find everything in God! We need nothing, we desire nothing. All we want is to obey His Will.

The one thing we need to do is to focus the mind on God, to live in constant awareness of His presence and dedicate our lives to Him! For God is the goal of our life, and He is to be realised, not merely discussed, defined, understood or explained.

Exercise:

Today, turn to God as often as you can. Think of Him during your daily routine. Pray to Him ever so often: "I love You God! I want to love You more and more! I want to love You more than anything else in the world. I want to love You to distraction, to intoxication. Grant me pure love and devotion for Thy Lotus Feet, and so bless me that this world-bewitching *maya* may not lead me astray. And make me, Blessed Master, an instrument of Thy help and healing in this world of suffering and pain."

The secret of a new life, the life beautiful, is love of God!